LETAROUILLY
ON
RENAISSANCE ROME

The Classical America Series in Art and Architecture

Henry Hope Reed and H. Stafford Bryant, Jr., General Editors

Architectural Book Publishing Company

*Student's Edition of the Monograph of the Work of
McKim, Mead & White, 1879–1915*
Architectural Rendering in Wash by H. Van Buren Magonigle
(in preparation)
The Architecture of Ancient Rome and of the Renaissance
by J. Buehlmann (in preparation)

With W. W. Norton & Company

The American Vignola by William R. Ware
The Architecture of Humanism by Geoffrey Scott
The Classic Point of View by Kenyon Cox
The Decoration of Houses by Edith Wharton and Ogden Codman, Jr.
The Golden City by Henry Hope Reed
Fragments from Greek and Roman Architecture
The Classical America Edition of Hector d'Espouy's Plates
Man As Hero: The Human Figure in Art by Pierce Rice (in preparation)
*Monumental Classic Architecture in Great Britain
and Ireland* by Albert E. Richardson
The Library of Congress: Its Architecture and Decoration by Herbert Small
What Is Painting? and Other Essays by Kenyon Cox (in preparation)
The New York Public Library: Its Architecture and Decoration
by Henry Hope Reed (in preparation)

CLASSICAL AMERICA is the society which encourages the classical tradition in the
arts of the United States. Inquiries about the society should be sent to Classical
America, in care of Architectural Book Publishing Company, 10 East 40th Street,
New York, N.Y. 10016

The Classical America Series in Art and Architecture

LETAROUILLY ON RENAISSANCE ROME

The Student's Edition of Paul Letarouilly's
Edifices de Rome Moderne
and *Le Vatican et la Basilique de Saint-Pierre*

BY
JOHN BARRINGTON BAYLEY

Edited by Henry Hope Reed
Preface by Arthur Ross
Biographical Notes by Nicholas King and Henry Hope Reed

CLASSICAL AMERICA

THE ARTHUR ROSS FOUNDATION

ARCHITECTURAL BOOK PUBLISHING COMPANY
New York

EDITOR'S ACKNOWLEDGEMENTS

The editor is grateful to the following for photographs: Mrs. Roberta Stothart of the J. Paul Getty Museum, Rogers Scudder, librarian of the American Academy in Rome, Mrs. Barbara Russell of the Smithsonian Institution, Gerald R. Blomeyer, Dick Schuler, Steven Miller, curator of Prints, Photographs, Drawings of the Museum of the City of New York, Edward Powis Jones, James Lees-Milne, and especially to Leonard Schurman of Rome. He would also like to thank Walter Persegati, il Segretario, Monumenti, Musei e Gallerie Ponteficie of the Vatican, Verena König, librarian of the Ecole française de Rome, Olivier Michel and Princess Nieves Massimo and Andrew Zaremba, Librarian of the Century Association for their help. For reviewing his editing of the manuscript he is indebted to Nicholas LeRoy King and his co-editor of the Classical America Series, H. Stafford Bryant, Jr.

Library of Congress Cataloging in Publication Data
Paul Letarouilly
*Letarouilly on Renaissance Rome: The Student's Edition of Paul Letarouilly's
Edifices de Rome moderne* and *Le Vatican et la basilique de
Saint-Pierre.* by John Barrington Bayley. (The Classical
America Series in Art and Architecture)

ISBN 8038-0950-0

CONTENTS

LIST OF ILLUSTRATIONS

XII. THE VATICAN

XIII. THE VATICAN—GREAT ROOMS

PREFACE

It was Paul Letarouilly, born in 1795—died in 1855, who, during the period of indecision and uncertainty following the defeat of Napoleon in 1815, turned Europe's architectural thought to a searching re-examination of the Italian Renaissance. A philosophical framework, sorely needed at that time in European history, found strength and inspiration in the classical principles. Similarly, the self-examination so prevalent in the closing decades of the 20th Century should lead us to seek and find a source of strength, a renewed confidence and a revival of our spirits as we, too, study the eternal verities so eloquently exemplified by the Italian Renaissance and preserved by Latarouilly.

In view of modern architecture's somewhat inadequate attempt to meet both the aesthetic and environmental needs of present-day society, an architectural form, less impersonal and more reassuring for the human spirit, is likely to bring about a renewed interest in Letarouilly's work. By means of accurate line exemplars, he has preserved for public study the important Renaissance monuments of the Sixteenth and Seventeenth Centuries in Rome. His immense labors were acclaimed throughout Europe and across the seas in the United States.

This volume was organized and undertaken by the late, distinguished, classical architect and scholar, John Barrington Bayley, in the attempt to extend the range of architectural thought during the current period of indecision. His untimely passing left an unfinished work which Classical America has undertaken to complete. It was not an easy task. *Edifices de Rome moderne* and *Le Vatican et la basilique de Saint-Pierre,* Letarouilly's two giant works, included more than 600 plates. It is hoped the reader will find in this volume a sweeping and revealing insight into the architectural principles and elegance of Renaissance Rome.

New York City   ARTHUR ROSS

BIOGRAPHICAL NOTES

Paul Letarouilly

Paul Letarouilly was born October 8, 1795, in the Norman town of Coutances, the eldest of ten children. His father had been a career staff officer in the royal army before the French Revolution and was later appointed superintendent of the military hospital established in the Breton capital of Rennes. By the time Paul was born, he had left military service and settled himself in business in Coutances. Through his acumen and energy he was able to provide his numerous family with an education which led his sons on to successful careers.

Paul attended the lycée at Rennes and arrived in Paris in the turbulent year of 1814, where he presented himself as a candidate for the famous Ecole Polytechnique. He was destined for a career as a military engineer, but the end of the Napoleonic Wars destroyed this impetus and he turned toward the field of architecture. Two years later he was accepted as a student in the atelier of the architect Charles Percier, and, later in 1816, he was admitted to the Ecole des Beaux Arts. He supported himself by working on the reconstruction of the neoclassic Odéon Theatre and graduated in 1820. That year Letarouilly set off for Italy—and his destiny.

Rome was the end of his journey. Although there was greatly renewed interest in the art of the ancients ever since the 1750s, the scale and power of Roman architecture was little appreciated and it overwhelmed the young Frenchman. Ancient Rome, he believed, was already sufficiently known and dealt with, but the classical heritage and expression of Renaissance Rome remained almost unknown, and on this expression his imagination and determination settled.

Letarouilly returned to Paris in 1824 and was named *inspecteur des travaux* at the Ministry of Finance which was going up along the rue de Rivoli. Later he was assigned to the rehabilitation of the Place de la Concorde and, in 1834, he received his

Fig. 1 Paul Letarouilly

major architectural commission, the renovation and expansion of the Collège de France on the rue St. Jacques near the Sorbonne. This was, aside from minor commissions from friends and family, his only architectural undertaking. The classical arches and courtyards of this building that are to be seen today were added by Letarouilly to the original college built by the *Ancien Régime* architect Chalgrin.

But Letarouilly's work in France was in all re-

Fig. 2 Courtyard of the Collège de France, Paris, 1831–1842, by Paul Letarouilly   *Photo Henry Hope Reed* II

spects secondary to his Italian vocation, and he returned to Italy in 1831 and again in 1844 for extended periods. He had undertaken no less a task than the systemization of the principles of design which lay behind the architecture of Rome in the 16th and 17th centuries. This meant, in other words, the work of Michelangelo, Sangallo, Ligorio, Peruzzi, Vignola, Bramante, Bernini, Fontana, della Porta, Maderno, Borromini—the great men who had converted the principles of classicism into the architecture of what was then called the modern age. His masterpiece, the great book of engraving known officially as *Edifices de Rome moderne, ou Receuil des palais, maisons, églises, couvents, autres monuments publics et particuliers les plus remarquables de la ville de Rome* took his entire life.

It was a magnificent production, consisting of 355 line drawings engraved on copper plates by the most skilled engravers available, in fact engravers who were brought up to the standards of their task by Letarouilly himself. Publication extended over many years, from 1825 to 1860 in fact, punctuated in the middle by the appearance of his celebrated map of Rome of 1841—in itself a masterpiece of engraving requiring five years of labor, and so detailed that it was used by the French Army in its siege of the city in 1848.

The *Edifices* was published in three volumes, each one centered on buildings of particular importance. In the first volume the Cancelleria was given 12 plates, for example, to the Farnese Palace 25 plates, and 17 to the Villa Giulia in the second, with 24 to the Massimi palaces and 9 to Santa Maria Maggiore in the third. With these went almost 800 quarto pages of notes and descriptions which, like the plates themselves, have proved an invaluable source for architects and historians over the years.

Besides the *Edifices* plates themselves, Letarouilly collected from sources all over Italy manuscripts and drawings of the Renaissance period which he treasured first as source material but later determined to share with the public through publication—which never came out. He also projected another vast work on St. Peter's and the Vatican. Some of these plates were engraved but the work as a whole remained unfinished in his lifetime.

This work on St. Peter's and the Vatican was as ambitious as the *Edifices*. Letarouilly's plan was to go back to the earliest Christian basilica when that part of Rome was largely occupied by the Circus of Nero and which was eventually the site of the modern Basilica of St. Peter. He was particularly anxious to set the complex and then very confused history of the construction of the great building straight and had already done considerable research on the subject in various libraries of the peninsula.

Letarouilly had also undertaken another important project, the publication of a popular edition of Roman architecture which would inform the public of his work and even raise money, through its sale, to finance his more erudite undertakings such as the *Edifices*. For this book he did a series of etchings based on Piranesi's views of Rome which were designed to illustrate a simplified text. Unfortunately even this project consumed too much money and had to be abandoned although well along toward completion.

All this labor took its toll on Letarouilly who dispensed money and energy alike, refusing lucrative commissions in order to bring his vast schemes to a fitting end. He cuts a somewhat austere figure, leading a life of sacrifice and abnegation, shunning social pleasures, absorbed in contemplation, brightening only when he discovered an unknown designer of a building, or when he found an explanation for a discrepancy of style, or when he took from the press a perfect impression of an engraving.

The world ignored him. Toward the end of his life, in 1851, the French Government thought to reward his talent and his dedication at the behest of friends by bestowing on him the Legion of Honor. His last years were saddened, indeed embittered, by the pirating of his work by a Belgian printer who turned out lithograph copies of his great engravings, almost as soon as they were printed. Copyright laws of those days could do nothing in such a case to protect the original artist. He died on October 25, 1855.

"Today, the effect of Letarouilly's immense labors can be seen in every capital city," writes an English critic, and indeed the *Edifices* became a major repository of design from the moment of its publication. His posthumously published *Le Vatican et la basilique de Saint-Pierre* (1882) in two volumes comprising 284 plates added to the wealth he had created. One senses, in the extraordinary elegance and purity of their plates, the inspiration, indeed the formation, of many of the architectural monuments of America. Certainly what is now known as the American Renaissance derives in considerable measure from the existence of his work, crystalizing as it does both the spirit and the fact of Rome's extraordinary artistic achievement.

NICHOLAS KING

FIG. 3 The New Wing of the Frick Collection, New York, 1977, designed by John Barrington Bayley *Photo Henry Hope Reed*. Courtesy of the Frick Collection.

John Barrington Bayley

John Barrington Bayley was that rarity in our time, a classical architect. He lived and breathed the grand tradition of Western art. This modest *Letarouilly on Modern Rome,* drawn from the great volumes of Paul Letarouilly, is very much part of the man for, to him, Rome was the center of the universe. His aim was to bring one of the more difficult aspects of the *Urbs*—difficult simply because of the sheer abundance of Renaissance Rome, not to mention a degree of quality which still sets it apart from all cities—within the horizon of the ordinary, educated person. This he did with an easy mixture of erudition, humor and conviction. The result is more than just a burst of light on a complex subject, it is a useful guide for anyone who goes to Rome.

Born in 1914 in Berkeley, California, he grew up in different cities as his father, an electrical engineer, was posted to places across the country. Among the schools he attended were the Chicago Latin, Harvey School, and South Kent in Connecticut. He went to Harvard, Class of 1937, and later the Harvard School of Design, Class of 1942. At the latter he was unknowingly in the wave of the Modern architects who were eventually to dominate the profession. What separated him from his fellows was his wide reading and a keen interest in our architectural heritage. A tour of duty in Paris during the war channelled his interest to the classical, and the inclination was reinforced by a four-year stay in Rome under the GI Bill, chiefly at the American Academy in Rome. In addition, he worked for the Department of State as architect in charge of the redecoration of our consulate in Florence and of our embassy, the Palazzo Margherita, in Rome.

Not surprisingly he was to have a part in the first exhibition after the war to offer the classical alternative. Presented at the Yale University Art Gallery in 1953 it was fittingly called *Ars in Urbe* as it unfolded the role of classical art in embellishing the city.

The next several decades he worked in New York. In 1957 and 1958 he exhibited classical projects under the titles, "New York Improved" and "Lin-

FIG. 4 The Ionic Order of the New Wing of the Frick Collection   *Photo Henry Hope Reed.* Courtesy of the Frick Collection.

coln Center Reconsidered." In 1963 he went to work for the Landmarks Preservation Commission of the City of New York where he remained, except for a brief interval, until 1972. While there he made the initial drawings for the Susan B. Wagner Wing of Gracie Mansion, the Mayor's Residence.

In the 1970s his great undertaking was the design for the new wing of the Frick Collection completed in 1977. Here his authoritative grasp of the classical achieved splendid fruition. An equal major work, although it remained on paper, was laying out the design for a new West Front to the United States Capitol.

He was a founder and first president of Classical America. He wrote for and edited the society's magazine, *Classical America,* and he wrote introductions for *The American Vignola* by William R. Ware and *The Decoration of Houses* by Edith Wharton and Ogden Codman, Jr. published, as is this volume of Letarouilly, in the Classical America Series in Art and Architecture. He died in Newport in December, 1981.

HENRY HOPE REED

XIV

I · THE ROMAN VISION

The purpose of this book is to put at your disposal, as Patrons and Artists, the gist of Letarouilly's work. A slice is enough. Rome's past is a *"selva oscura,"* Dante's dark forest, where I could almost say that everyone loses his way. Letarouilly could not stop; and it took thirty years to engrave his drawings onto copper plates for the six volumes of this work.

Everything being ineluctably of its own time, Letarouilly's plates have a distinctly neat and linear First Empire look to them. His taste was formed in the office of Percier and Fontaine who invented the Empire Style. Letarouilly's facades would do nicely for the Rue de Rivoli (fig. 1), by Percier and Fontaine. Its arches, window surrounds, belt course and cornices are straight Italian Renaissance, i.e., Letarouilly, with the difference that they and the walls carrying them are in tightly-cut French limestone. In Rome the walls are colored with stucco, and the rest is travertine, a coarser stone lending itself to a broader, more sculptural treatment. The Italian Renaissance was very much "en vogue" when Letarouilly left for Rome in 1821.

In the first sentence of this introduction I put Patrons in front of Artists which includes architects. Patrons are much more important. Talent is a natural resource, and there is always plenty of it. But how is it to be put to use? The Bible says ". . . Many are called, but few are chosen." In great epochs more are chosen, and they accomplish more. Talent is fully employed.

The chief role in art, let me repeat, is that of the Patron. All he has to do is pay for what he wants, and talent will produce it. It is very much in the classical vein, which is supremely objective, to be putting art with money. Art, ineffable and subjective, is for intellectuals.

Let us look at the patrons of yesteryear. Western Art, the Graeco-Roman Judeo-Christian continuum, was paid for, in the main, by aged ecclesiastics, then came kings and nobles, married often times to burgher money, and then the thalassocrats, the sea rulers, of Venice, Genoa, Amsterdam, et al. These last, as fellow republics, help us in that they show that historically art does not require a monarchical order where throne and altar are united. Oligarchical peaks do just as well.

Washington and Jefferson and many of the "pater patriae" were patrons. They were keepers of the garden, Adams before the Fall. They had the classical vision, the vision of some Golden Age. Without this vision classical art fails.

Jefferson spent many delightful days in the Ro-

Fig. 1 Rue de Rivoli, Paris, 1811–1835, by Percier and Fontaine. Photo Henry Hope Reed II

1

FIG. 2 The Maison Carrée, Nîmes, France, 14 A.D. Courtesy Warder Collection

FIG. 3 Pont du Gard, Nîmes, France. 19 B.C. Photo John Barrington Bayley

man ruins of Provence, especially at Nîmes. There he "fell in love with the Maison Carrée," the best preserved Roman temple existing (fig. 2). He gazed on the Pont du Gard (fig. 3) the most impressive of aqueducts, and the amphitheater at Nîmes with seats for twenty-thousand spectators, explored the "Temple" of Diana, a staircase hall which dignified the approach to some paths at higher level, and was filled, he tells us, with awe and admiration for the nation which conceived and carried to completion such works. How pleasant to think of our third President in such suitable surroundings.

Washington served quite as well as Jefferson as a model patron. Improvements never ceased at his beloved Mount Vernon. The serpentine paths in the garden, the first in America, were laid out during the Revolution.

The Vanderbilts were the only great American family with the "manie de bâtir," they built sixty-five large houses. But this mania does not necessarily involve one in "la folie des grandes maisons" or the Grand Manner, it can be on the most modest scale. Anybody can have a vision of a Golden Age.

I refer to "a" Golden Age. The backward glance

FIG. 4 Place de la Concorde, Paris, 1749–1753, by Ange-Jacques Gabriel. Photo French Government Tourist Office

FIG. 5 East Front of the Louvre, Paris, 1667–1674, by Claude Perrault. Photo Henry Hope Reed II

FIG. 6 The West Front of the United States Capitol. Photo Katherine Russell

transforms, and classical art is always retrospective. Ange-Jacques Gabriel said that when he was building the Place de la Concorde (fig. 4) he was building in the manner of the Grand Siècle. He modelled the facades there on Perrault's east front for the Louvre (fig. 5). The facades both have long colonnaded porches set on a ground floor "en avant-corps," both have dramatic entablatures crowned with balustrades, but there the resemblance stops. We are more struck by the way they differ. Bramante's project for St. Peter's seems like a hodge-podge to us, and yet he said that he was putting the Pantheon on top of the Basilica of Maxentius.

One's vision of a Golden Age is really aimed at national achievement. One would like to see the Mall in Washington without the Modern buildings which have disfigured it in recent years. I would like to see the United States Capitol re-fronted (figs. 6–8). I worked on the drawings for this. One day someone phoned: "What are you doing Bayley?" "I'm working on a new facade. It's sixty feet high and six hundred feet long, and all marble." Moment of hubris.

The purpose of the construction would be to create a fitting conclusion to the Mall. The exterior details were fixed. We followed extactly the models

FIG. 7 John Barrington Bayley's design for a new West Front to the United States Capitol

of Thornton, Bulfinch, Latrobe and Walter. For the interior I proposed, frivolously—but one should never say no to any possibility of striking a blow for classical beauty and majesty; you never know, some vestige of your design may survive—a suite of rooms which would have divided off into several meeting rooms on occasion. The suite would have been behind the porch of the central block. It would have been a *grand gallery* opening out onto the porch through round-headed Bulfinch windows, and looking down the Mall to the hazy hills of Virginia and the far gleaming pediment of Arlington House. A magnificent gallery, glittering with gilt and mirrors in the style of Latrobe, with one of the world's most splendid views. It would have been useful on state occasions. It would have been reached from the East Front by the great exterior staircase. Then the great domed rotunda. Then the Bulfinch corridor, down which one would, as one approached the gallery, see the obelisk of the Washington Monument. It would have been one of the great classical ensembles.

For the outside the script, as I have said, was fixed. For the great gallery I would have turned to Letarouilly's Pietro Massimo Palace (Ch. V, plate 13) and used it as a prototype and gradually have worked through that to give the room the Federal character of Latrobe who, I feel, is an architect simply beyond praise. I would pay tribute to him. Alas, this does not seem to be the moment for great classical affirmations, but designs once they are made have a way of happening eventually.

The Vision of the Golden Age, however febrile, is an attempt to impose cosmos on chaos. Cosmos is from the Greek roots to "arrange, adorn, having the power to beautify" and "of or belonging to the universal considered as an ordered system."

How is this Vision to be established? How is the seed of the acanthus, the immortal morphological symbol of the West as the lotus is of the East, to be planted? Rome is the place to begin. The Roman Forum is too difficult to comprehend. I would recommend the Colosseum (Ch.III, fig.1) for the first step, followed by the study of the Five Orders and ancient ornament and, last, the great palaces and churches. Figure 1 of Chapter III is reproduced from plate 122 of Hector d'Espouy's *Fragments from Greek and Roman Architecture* published as is this book, in the Classical America Series in Art and Architecture. The Orders are spelled out in William R. Ware's *The American Vignola*. Letarouilly follows as guide to Renaissance Rome. All three books, as most in the Series, have been produced under the patronage of the Arthur Ross Foundation.

That Letarouilly has served Americans before, we know by glancing at the *Student's Edition of the Monograph of the Work of McKim, Mead & White*, yet another volume in the Series made possible by the Arthur Ross Foundation. We have to look to the palaces and the churches as did the patrons and the artists of the turn of the century. The Vision of the Golden Age begins there.

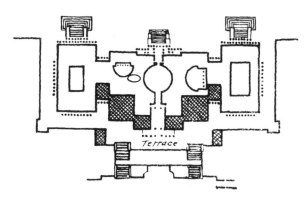

FIG. 8 Plan by John Barrington Bayley for the new West Front of the United States Capitol. The additions are cross-hatched.

II · SQUARES

It is proper to begin with the square of the Capitol, the Campidoglio, found on the crown of the Capitoline Hill (plate 1 and fig. 1). A sacred citadel in ancient times with its Temple of Jupiter Optimus Maximus, it was the symbolic center of the Roman Empire, the terminus of the Sacred Way which came through the Forum. It became and it remains the seat of the secular government of the city. At the center of its square stands the equestrian statue of Marcus Aurelius, a symbol of Rome's continuity.

In the fifteenth century it was unfinished, described in 1431 by Poggio Bracciolini as "a rubbish heap and a tip for dung. . ." The Senatorial Palace, today the City Hall, the noblest and the oldest, had formed the background for several centuries (fig. 2). On the right was the Palace of the Conservators, a very simple structure (fig. 3).

In 1538, by command of Pope Paul III (Farnese), the statue of Marcus Aurelius was moved here from the Lateran Palace and Michelangelo began to make plans for the square and its buildings. He designed the façade of the Senatorial Palace, the noblest and oldest of the Capitoline buildings. To the right is the Palace of the Conservators which he converted from a plain to a noble structure, and duplicated it with a design for the Capitoline Museum to the north. Like the Senatorial Palace the buildings, the square, the Cordonata, a road with steps leading to the square, were not completed or built until after his death.

We notice immediately (plate 2) that all three buildings are supplied with colossal pilasters. The colossal pilaster goes through any number of stories from the pedestal to the entablature. Here the giant order made its bow in a secular building (fig. 4). It provides a solution to the problem which had occupied architects since Leon Battista Alberti, of how to combine the ancient system of columns, pilasters, and cornices with the division of stories in a modern palace, with its windows set on string courses, in such a way as to insure a support for a cornice proportioned to the whole building, and not just the pilasters of the top floor. The material employed for the supporting members differs from the walls, that is, travertine for pilasters, pier strips, columns and cornices, and brick for the walls. Michelangelo treated the ground floor of the Senatorial Palace as the rusticated base for the giant order with the pilasters and other supporting elements were applied to the existing building.

The extremely heavy entablatures and balustrades of the Capitoline Museum and the Palace of the Conservators are of Michelangelesque proportions. A great deal of heed should be given to this device. The eye, of course, tends to reduce their height when seen from the ground. If a building looks well proportioned when it is drawn up in an elevation, then you are wrong. It will look weak to the spectator, and this is a common fault in most American colonial buildings.

I noticed when I was working on St. Paul's Chapel in lower Manhattan that an elevation of the tower looks very top heavy, and yet when seen from the ground the effect is very fine (fig. 5).

Michelangelo suggests the presence of a structural logic which, by being at the same time denied, makes the effect of the entire design enigmatic. His knowing disrespectful attitude towards the Orders also underlies his invitation of the colossal order, used for the first time on the Palace of the Conservators (plate 3). In this design the column is reduced to a minor supporting role, while the pilaster is blown up to become the major visual element now adopted to make the facade act as a place 'to

FIG. 1 Elevation of the principal buildings on the Capitoline (Campidoglio): The Capitoline Museum, The Senatorial Palace (City Hall of modern Rome), and the Palace of the Conservators, 1540–1644, by Michelangelo. From Georges Gromort, *Eléments d'architecture classique*

FIG. 2 The Senatorial Palace, ca. 1530, before it was transformed by Michelangelo. Cabinet des Dessins, Musée du Louvre

FIG. 3 Palace of the Conservators, ca. 1530, before it was rebuilt following the design of Michelangelo. Cabinet des Dessins, Musée du Louvre

shape the space of the square, and to make clearly visible the similarity of design that links all three buildings on the square.

The three buildings give the square, a trapezoid in plan, an unmistakable aura. In particular the two symmetrical ones seem to have between them an aulic or court-like enclosed atmosphere which might almost be described as that of a great salon.

Fig. 5 Tower and steeple of St. Paul's Church, New York, 1796, by James Crommelin Lawrence. *Photo Dick Schuler*

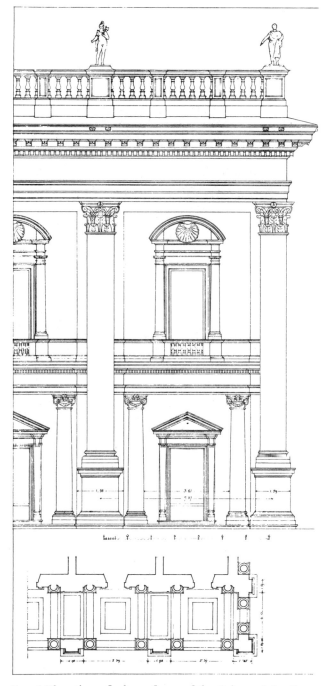

Fig. 4 Elevation of a bay of one of the Palace of the Conservators and the Capitoline Museum. From Georges Gromort, *Eléments d'architecture classique*

The symmetrical ones also have open porticos, a perfect half-inside, half outside treatment (plate 3). The porticos screen various entrances and eliminate a cross-axis for the main doorway. Were they not present, that is, were they solid, there would have been a feeling of constriction in the square.

In reality the square is designed as a terrace. A decisive screen was needed, not to lose, not to contradict, the desired effect of terraced height. A balustrade being insufficient, the circa eighteen-foot ancient statues of the Dioscuri, Castor, tamer of horses, and Pollux, god as a boxer, were placed here. It is fitting that the hero twins, sons of Jupiter and Leda, be on the Capitoline because they rescued Rome at the Battle of Lake Regullus in 496 B.C.

FIG. 6 So-called Trophies of Marius on the Capitoline by Antoine-Martin Garnaud.
From Hector d'Espouy's *Fragments from Greek and Roman Architecture*

FIG. 7 Statue of Marcus Aurelius on a base by Michelangelo. In the background left, the Senatorial Palace, right, Palace of the Conservators. Photo John Barrington Bayley

To either side of them are the so-called Trophies of Marius (fig. 6) from a triumphal arch of the time of the Emperor Domitian in the first century. Then there are two columns, milestones from Via Appia, and the statues of Constantine the Great and his son, Constantine II.

The same care given this screen was also afforded the balustrades of the long access ramp, the Cordonata. Near the top they are set further apart, thus helping to give a person walking up a slight feeling of expansion accompanying the sensation of ascent. An almost imperceptible sense of lightness and greater nobility is slowly infused.

The statues are, of course, an essential ingredient to the Roman setting. At the foot of the Senatorial Palace are the colossal river gods, the Nile and the Tiber (formerly the Tigris). Between them in a niche is a porphyry statue of the seated Minerva. There is the bronze wolf of the Capitol seen in plate 2 behind the preceptor and his circle of pupils dressed à la Raphael. It is a work of the sixth century B.C. The twins were added in the fifteenth century by Antonio di Pallaiolo. (The original statue is now in the Palace of the Conservators and its im-

Fig. 8 View of the Capitoline showing Michelangelo's plan for the pavement of the square. Dated 1569, and executed by Etienne Dupérac. Photo Cabinet des Estampes, Bibliothèque Nationale

itation is now on the other flank of the Senatorial Palace.)

> And thou, the thunder-stricken* nurse of Rome!
> She-wolf! whose brazen-imaged dugs impart
> The milk of conquest yet within the dome,
> Where, as a monument of antique art
> Thou standest: mother of the mighty heart.
>
> Byron, *Childe Harold*

At the opposite end, as it were, at the foot of the Cordonata are two lions, part of two small fountains. "You must by no means neglect to look at the two lions of Egyptian marble who spout water of their mouths," advised Sir Joshua Reynolds of the pair which are actually of black Egyptian granite. "They screw up their mouths for that purpose, as a man does when he whistles, among the best antiques of their kind in Rome."

I have saved for the last the most important statue of all, the Marcus Aurelius (fig. 7) in the center of the square. "As the most majestic representation of the kingly character that the world has ever seen, it was the model for all Renaissance equestrian statues," Nathaniel Hawthorne observed, "A sight of

*Cicero spoke of the statue having been struck by lightning in his time.

the old heathen emperor is enough to create an evanescent sentiment of loyalty even in a democratic bosom, so august does he look, so fit to rule, so worthy of man's profoundest homage and obedience, so inevitably attractive of his love. He stretches forth his hand with an air of profound magnificence and unlimited authority, as if uttering a decree from which no appeal was permissible, but in which the obedient subject would find his highest interests consulted; a command that was in itself a benediction."

When the statue came here, Paul III had Michelangelo design the base. In addition, the Master drew a plan for the square, consisting of an oval, slightly sunken on its perimeter reached by three steps and rising in the center to the statue base. The surface was given a geometric pattern (fig. 8). Instead, the pattern, as shown on Figure 9, was built. Michelangelo's design did not replace it until 1940, the pattern reproduced in the 1569 engraving of Duperac but with two not three descending steps. A further change was made to interrupt the oval by removing the steps at four places, two at the top and two at the bottom of the oval, to permit cars to cross the square from access streets.

9

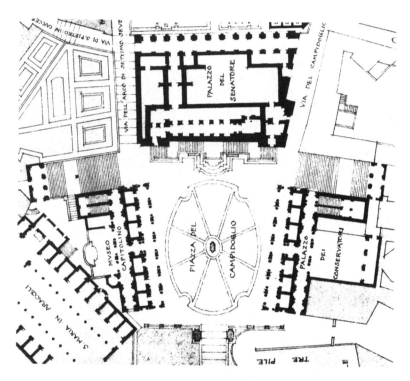

Fig. 9 Plan of the Capitoline showing the original pavement of the square, replaced by that of Michelangelo. From Georges Gromort, *Eléments d'architecture classique*

PLATE 1. View of the Square and the Buildings of the Capitoline (Campidoglio). In the background is the Senatorial Palace, to the right the Palace of the Conservators, to the left, the Capitoline Museum, and in the middle, the equestrian statue of Marcus Aurelius.

11

PLATE 2. View of the Senatorial Palace, today's City Hall, on the right. Directly on the left is the Palace of the Conservators and, beyond it, the Capitoline Museum. The steps in the background lead to the Church of Santa Maria in Ara-Coeli.

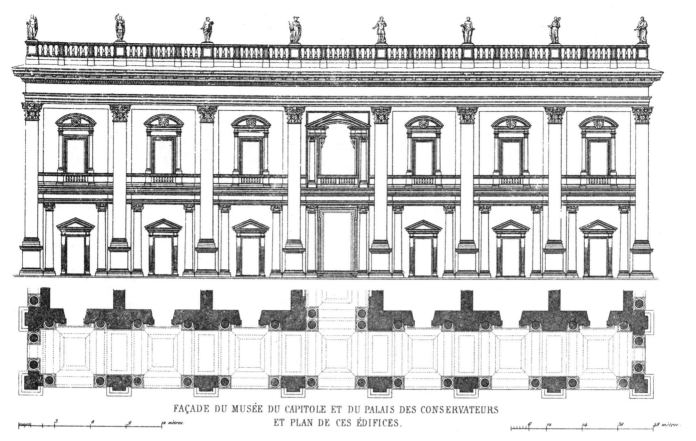

FAÇADE DU MUSÉE DU CAPITOLE ET DU PALAIS DES CONSERVATEURS
ET PLAN DE CES ÉDIFICES.

PLATE 3. The Facade of the Palace of the Conservators and the Capitoline Museum with a Plan of the Portico.

View of the Square from the Portico of the Palace of the Conservators.

Fɪɢ. 1 Part of the facade of the Colosseum. Wash drawing by Louis Duc.
From Hector d'Espouy, *Fragments from Greek and Roman Architecture*

III · COURTYARDS

Internal courts have never found much favor with us. It is an Anglo-Saxon attitude. But is it? In any case this would not apply to our Sun Belt or California where, in fact, there are missions with wonderful courtyards. Missions or monastic houses were based on the Roman country house. The first monasteries were actually established in ancient Roman country houses. They centered about the peristyle, and this became the cloister.

The whole point of a court surrounded by columns, that is colonnades, is that it gives access to many rooms without having corridors, as we see in the example here. It also provides a focus for the institution where people see each other, where there is a place for fountains and statues. Designs for the superimposed arcades were based largely on the Colosseum (fig. 1) or the Theatre of Marcellus (fig. 2).

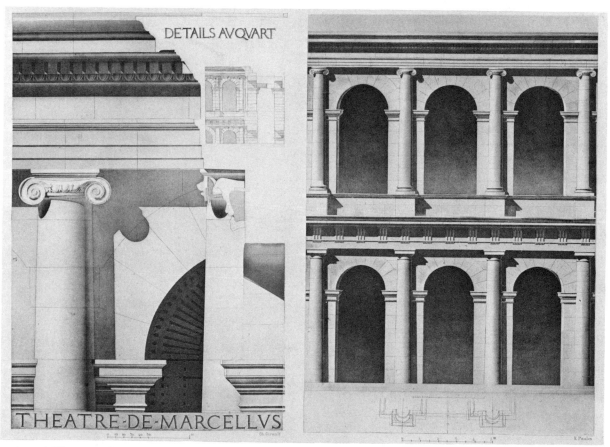

FIG. 2 Theatre of Marcellus. Wash drawings, details by Charles Girault and elevation by Edmond Paulin. From Hector d'Espouy, *Fragments from Greek and Roman Architecture*

FIG. 3 Courtyard of the Freer Gallery in Washington, Charles Adams Platt architect.
Photo Courtesy of the Freer Gallery of Art, Smithsonian Institution, Washington, D.C.

Ancient Roman buildings turned their backs on the world. If you look at a map of ancient Rome you will see the forum, a central open space usually surrounded by public buildings and colonnades and used as a market or general meeting place, a space carved out of a congery of streets and buildings. The space is colonnaded about its perimeter, and in the space are freestanding basilicas and temples. Most Roman buildings were not freestanding; they abut each other, so there were no major exterior elevations. The baths and palaces did not have facades. It was the interiors, the rooms and courts, which were magnificent.

Washington has many courts but, even in the Federal Triangle, they are plain and utilitarian. The Freer Gallery of Art (fig. 3) has a very fine interior court; it has, however, only one story.

Now that our national taste for extreme densities—megatowers and great lumps like the Health and Human Services Building (fig. 4) on Independence Avenue south of the Mall—is passing,

perhaps our patrons can be persuaded to consider buildings with more focus and less destiny, and with great courts.

FIG. 4 Health and Human Services Building, Washington, D.C. Photo Catherine A. Russell

16

The courtyard of the Sapienza or College of Wisdom (plate 1) is a model of its kind. (It takes its name from the motto over the window above the main entrance—initium sapientiae timor Domini—the fear of the Lord is the beginning of Wisdom.) It has a great effect of dignity and beauty which strikes one immediately. This is derived from the proportions of the arches (plate 2). One notes that the arches of the *piano nobile,* the second floor, are somewhat higher than on the ground floor, and that the entablature of the *piano nobile* is much deeper than usual (plate 3), and the pedestal lower. The balusters are pedestal height. I might point out that the baluster is a Renaissance invention. The first balusters we know of are in the choir loft of the Sistine Chapel, c. 1484; balusters did not exist in antiquity.

Where the secret of this court's excellence lies I cannot say. I suspect that the reveals, the depth of the piers behind the pilasters, has something to do with it. As soon as that is said one thinks it is the proportions of the whole court and so it ". . . gave you time to puzzle out, if you could," wrote Henry James, "the essence of the insolent secret. It was all really, with the very swagger of simplicity, a matter of . . . the mutual relation of parts."

The courtyard of the Mattei Palace (plate 4) is the court of a dwelling. It is famous for its incrustations of Antique fragments and statues. How strange it is that Rome should be so full of the silent audience of statues, the finest ornament there, and that there should be so few elsewhere. Emperors, gods, athletes, heroes, vestals, matrons, maids, the whole range of mythology, history and the taxonomy of the human form divine. Statues about one third over life size are the perfect ornament. Notice that here there is a statue at the base of every pilaster. On Michelangelo's Capitoline buildings we saw them on the pedestals between the balustrades, silhouetted against the sky. Statues are the highest form of ornament.

On the *piano nobile* of the court at either end of the balustrades between the arches we can see busts. These busts, in point of fact, are about thrice life size. The colossal has great drama, we are always glad to see it. The Periclean Greeks seldom used it. I can think only of their votive statues; Zeus or Athena within the cellas of their temples. The Romans acquired a taste for the colossal from the Hellenistic Greeks, the heirs of Alexander the Great. The Colossus of Rhodes comes to mind, as does the Pergamon Altar, now in Berlin (fig. 5).

FIG. 5 The Altar of Zeus at Pergamon, 197–159 B.C., now in the Pergamon Museum, Berlin. Photo Courtesy Gerald R. Blomeyer

One sometimes hears it said "But Roman sculpture is so bad. Greek is better." Greek sculpture is unsurpassed, and all sculpture for Rome and the Empire was made by Greeks. In Renaissance Rome many antique statues were restored, for restoration is an art. Today's enthusiasm for a genuine fragment approaches abstraction, and also it makes of a statue not something to be used, but a specimen like a butterfly on a pin, something for the culture maven.

The first work of Bramante in Rome was the small court of the cloister of Santa Maria della Pace. Here, at the ground level (plate 5) you can see arches resting on piers with an applied pilaster. It is more Antique, more Roman at the Cancelleria (see below). The pier is considered as a Doric Order, the impost moldings are the equivalent of a modified capital at the top of a pilaster. This capital at the back of the pier he projected onto the inner wall to carry a quadripartite groin vault where it becomes a cornice.

On the *piano nobile* (plate 6) he placed columns over the centers of the arches beneath and this was criticized at the time, as were the very small support of the entablature and the quarter pilaster of the corners. At the corner I find the rather slim pier—on the diagonal it appears no wider than the other piers—to be judicious for this small court.

The top entablature breaks forward above the pilasters (plate 7). Over the Corinthian capitals are double corbels. The corbels are an enrichment, as Bramante could see at the Colosseum, of the frieze.

The Cancelleria or the Chancellery, one of Rome's

17

FIG. 6 The Villard Mansions at Madison Avenue and 50th Street, New York. 1883 by McKim, Mead & White. Photo Dick Schuler

largest palaces, was substantially completed when Bramante arrived in Rome in 1493. Built of travertine quarried from the Colosseum, it is huge being 300 feet long and proportionally high so that it was necessary to break the vast mass of the masonry both horizontally and vertically (plate 8). The ground floor is set on a high podium which has small windows to light the basement. Above it, the facades rise in three tiers, the lowest in channelled masonry and the two upper each ornamented with plain Corinthian pilasters arranged in alternative spacings instead of the regular spacings of earlier astylar palaces. The intermediate full entablature is subdued while that at the top has vertical modillion across the frieze giving it all the vigor of the crowning cornice of the Colosseum. The shallow pilasters stand on simulated pedestals, the corresponding "blind" parapets serving as aprons to the main windows. These last have arched openings on the *piano nobile* fitted within square heads. The square heads have projecting cornices and paterae between the arches and cornices. This is a form used in Antiquity and adopted here for the first time. The top floor is similar but the windows are smaller and have small round headed attic windows over them. The rustication is even all the way up; no attempt was made to give it a more massive air on the ground floor by heavier rustication as in Florence.

(Two buildings in New York City show influence of the Cancelleria, the Villard Houses, by McKim, Mead & White, now part of the Helmsley Palace Hotel at Madison Avenue and 49th Street (fig. 6), and the Convent of the Sacred Heart, formerly the Otto Kahn residence, by G. Armstrong Stenhouse on Fifth Avenue and 91st Street (fig. 7). The latter appears to be a closer model because its facades are made of St. Maximin limestone from France which resembles Roman travertine.)

This description is only by way of an introduction to the courtyard, very much part of the subject of this chapter. The Roman solution as against the Florentine, derives from the Colosseum (fig. 1) or the Theatre of Marcellus (fig. 2). The cortile or courtyard is 103 feet 6 inches by 63 feet and 6 inches surrounded by superimposed arcades (plate 9). For both the Order is Doric with the capitals of the *piano nobile* (plates 10 and 11) somewhat more elaborate of the two; they have bands of leaves below the necking and a circlet of rosettes in the spandrels alluding to the armorial bearing of Cardinal Riario, builder of the palace.

The topmost story is of masonry, spans two tiers of small windows and carries a cornice similar to that adopted on the front. Corinthian pilasters divide the space between the superimposed windows. In this the third story follows the Colosseum.

FIG. 7 The Convent of the Sacred Heart, former Otto Kahn mansion, on Fifth Avenue and 91st Street, New York. 1914–1918 by G. Armstrong Stenhouse. Photo Dick Schuler

18

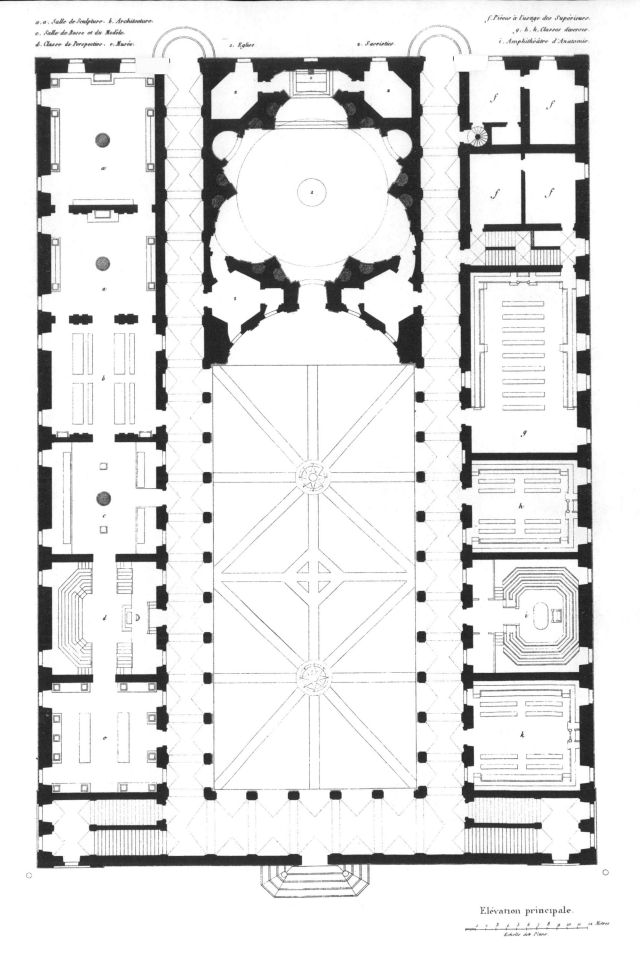

Elévation principale.

Echelle des Plans.

Plate 1. Plan of the Court of the Sapienza

19

Coupe sur la longueur de la Cour.

Echelle des Plans.

PLATE 2. View of the Court of the Sapienza

20

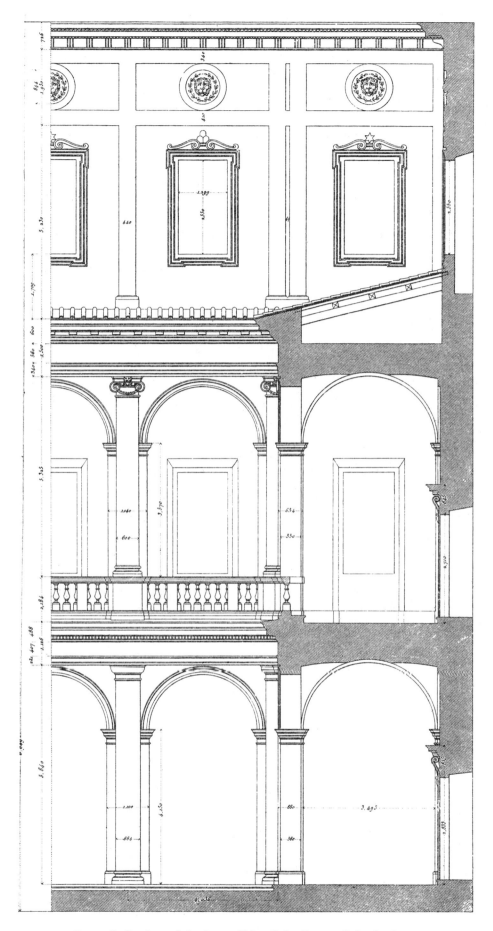

PLATE 3. Section of the Long Side of the Court of the Sapienza

21

PLATE 4. The Courtyard of the Mattei Palace

PLATE 5. The Cloister of Santa Maria della Pace by Bramante

23

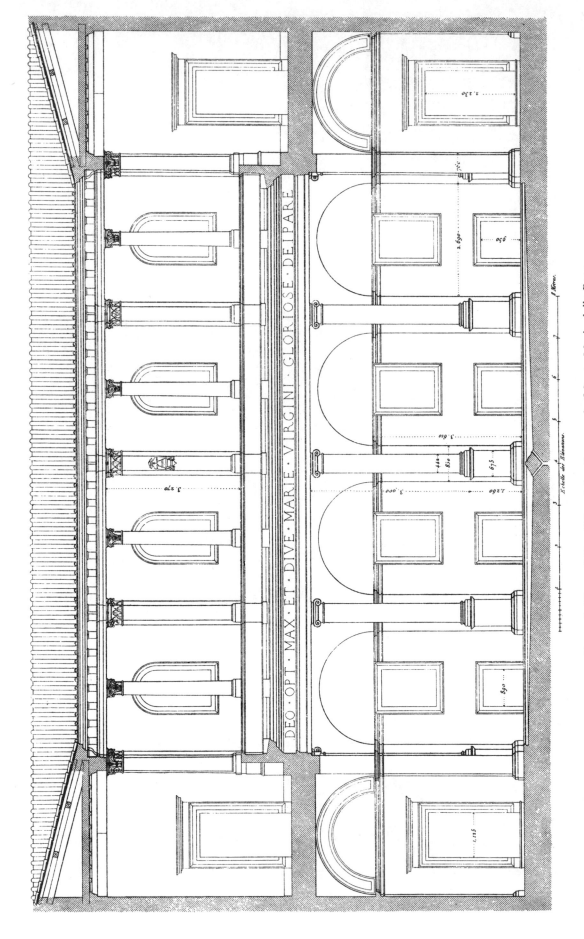

Plate 6. View of One Side of the Courtyard of Santa Maria della Pace

24

D · OPT · MAX ·

Imposte des arcades du rez-de-chaussée.

Base du piédestal de l'ordre ionique.

Croisée sous le portique du rez-de-chaussée.

Porte sous le portique du rez-de-chaussée.

PLATE 7. Details of the Two Orders of the Courtyard of Santa Maria della Pace

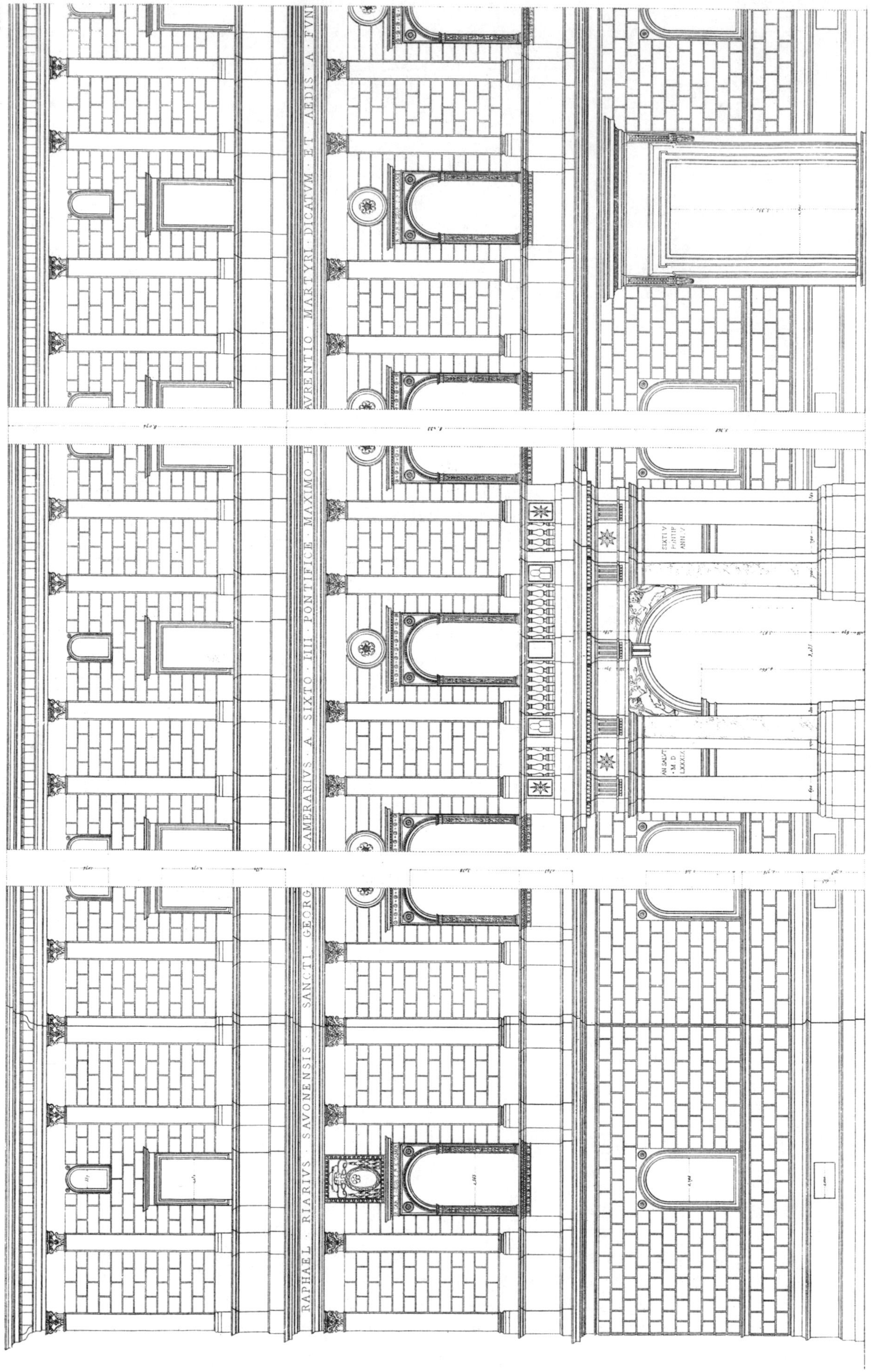

Pl. 80

RAPHAEL · RIARIVS · SAVONENSIS · SANCTI · GEORG · CAMERARIVS · A · SIXTO · IIII · PONTIFICE · MAXIMO · H · AVRENTIO · MARTYRI · DICATVM · ET · AEDIS · A · FVND

AN · SALVT · M · D · LXXXIX

SIXTI · V · PONTIF · ANN · /

Escala de Palmos · Escala de Vicenza

PLATE 8. The Principal Facade of the Chancellery

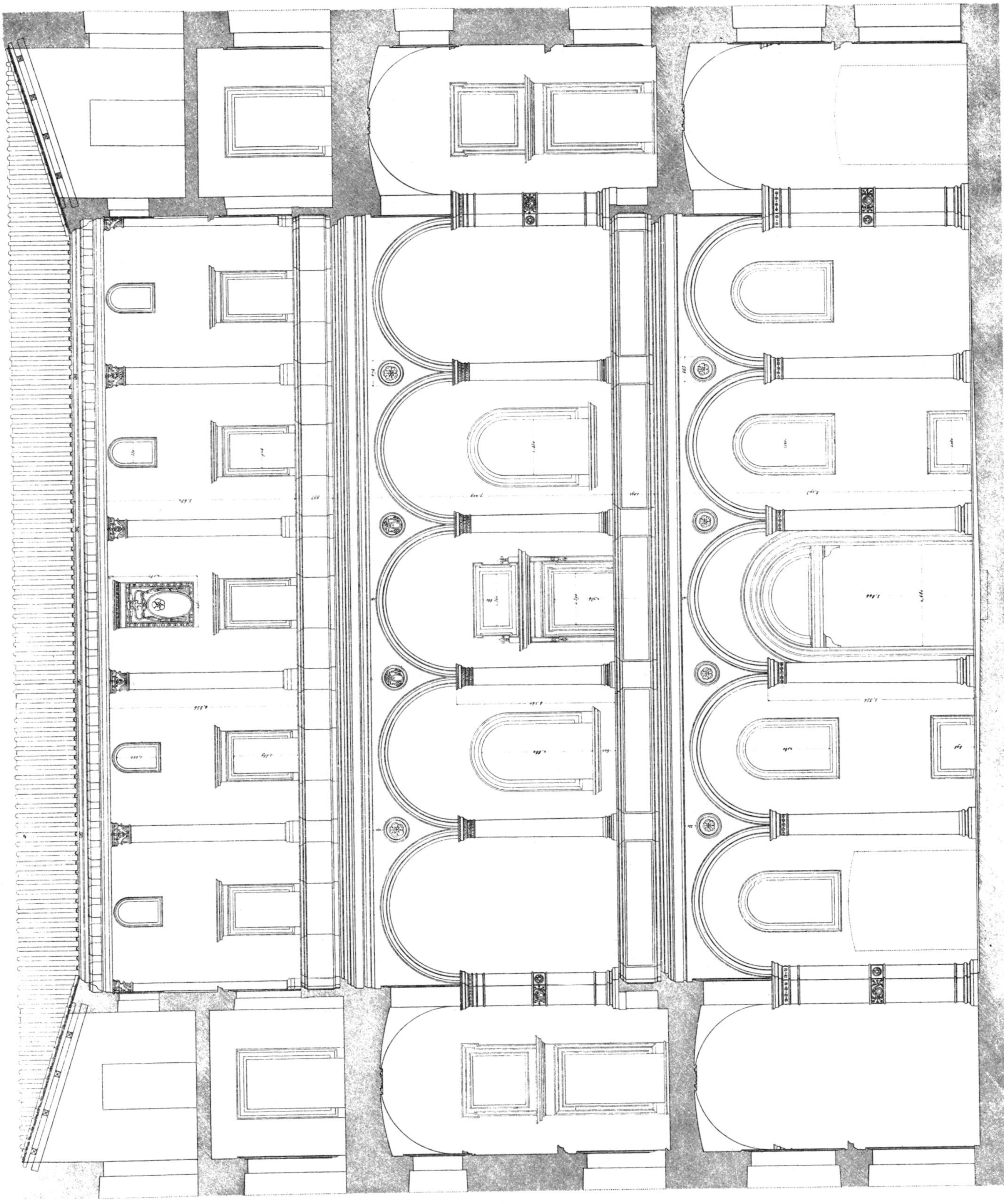

PLATE 9. The Elevation of a Side of the Court of the Chancellery

PLATE 10. View of the Court from the Portico of the Ground Floor of the Chancellery

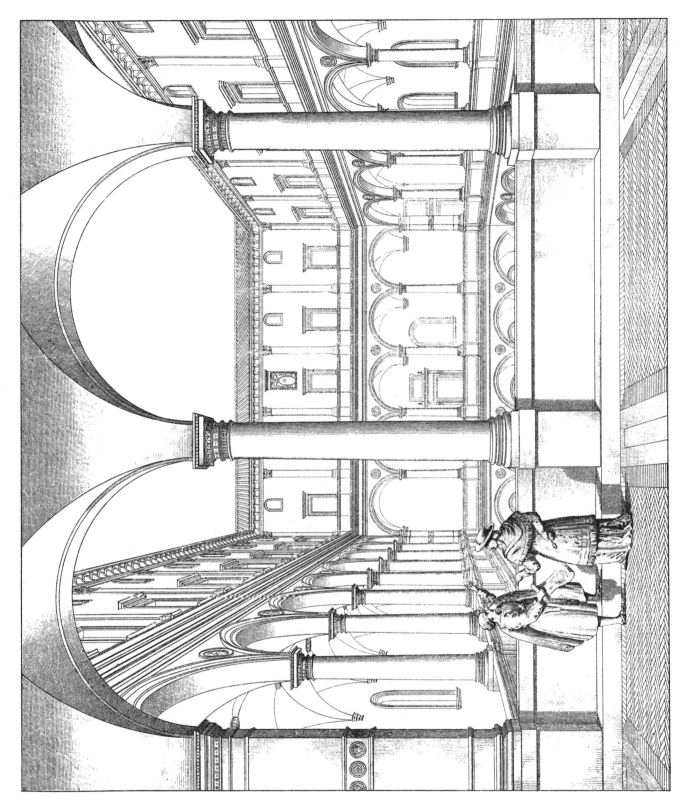

PLATE 11. *View of the Court from the Portico of the* Piano Nobile *or Second Floor of the Chancellery*

IV · PALACES

"Palace," palazzo, palacio, palais, palast, all these words have a Palatine (one of the Seven Hills of Rome and site of the imperial residence) ring. Also, palazzo really is and always has been an apartment house. All Continental European cities are based on it with the exception of Amsterdam, other cities of the Low Countries and possibly parts of Scandinavia and the Germanies. Let us say that all cities of the Imperium Romanum are based on the "palazzo." In Paris or Rome, cities best known to us, we go into the building by way of a *portone/portail* which is vehicular, past a *portiere/concièrge* to one side of the big vehicular entrance double-doors, one of them set with a little door for people, is the staircase. This by easy gradient mounts to the *piano nobile* or *bel étage* where rich people live and where the ceilings are high. It then mounts to another floor where there are professionals, *noblesse de robe* and lesser lights and finally ends with added stories and generally rooftop dwellings, modifications, not shown in Letarouilly's views. The "palazzo" is a multi-class dwelling. We do not have rich and poor neighborhoods but rather rich and poor levels, and everyone passes on the stairway.

Let us take a look at the plates we have furnished. The first "palazzo," the little Spada palace (plate 1) is "classique," a palace with shops on the street and a corridor back to the staircase and court, *bel étage*, etc. This is essentially also the ancient Roman formula, and similar palazzi can be seen in model form based on remains at Ostia. It is also close to the Rue de Rivoli in Paris.

Let us "parse" the facade. The arches would have been filled with wooden shop fronts and counters; over the shops, reached by a little staircase, is a low-ceiling dwelling room, *"piano ammezzato,"* or cut down, for the shopkeeper family looks out of the squared window over the arch. All the window frames rest on belt courses. The *portone* is rusticated with Tuscan pilasters and archivolt and a Corinthian entablature with the modillions and dentils omitted. The *piano nobile* has a Corinthian Order with pilasters and entablature. Over this is an attic with a belt course for the window frames of the top story. The window frames of the "piano nobile" have an architrave with a frieze and cornice, an entablature. The frames on the top floor have "Greek ears (*or crossettes*)."

Where a squarish window (plates 2 and 3) is to be seen over a high window it can mean that there is a *"piano ammezzato,"* or that, and this gladdens the heart of the passerby, the room is two stories high and at night one glances up through the upper window to catch a glimpse of a frescoed ceiling.

The Palazzo Muti (plate 2) stands at the end of a long narrow square. It would make a splendid townhouse. It is about the width of three New York City lots. It is where Bonnie Prince Charlie spent his last days.

This palace near the Piazza della Pace (plate 4) somehow has the look of an invention especially at the top floor. It recalls some of Poussin's architecture, and perhaps a little bit of Ledoux and Boullée.

House on Via del Governo Vecchio (plate 5). Here again the top floors appear inventive, which is not to dismiss them in any way. We are concerned here not with archaelogy but architecture. The floors below look very real, and the shops with their counters could be straight from Pompeii. Private houses (plates 6 and 7) are scarce as hen's teeth in Rome, but they do exist, and since we are the Anglo-American market, I have included as many as possible.

PLATE 1. Facade of the Little Spada Palace on Via di Capo di Ferro

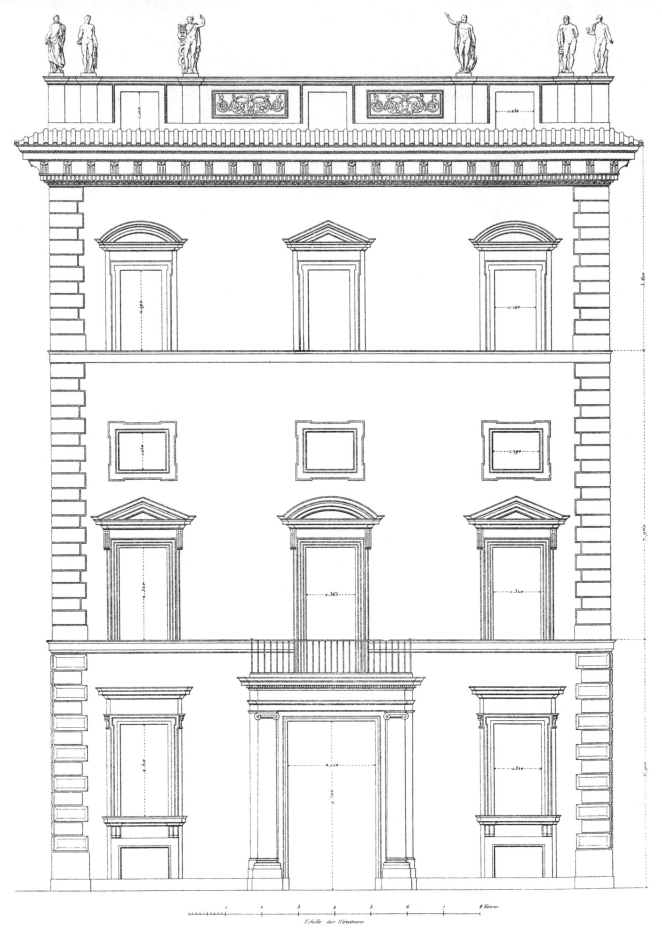

PLATE 2. Facade of the Muti Papazzurri Palace in the Piazza di SS. Apostoli

32

PLATE 3. Facade of the Casa Professa de' Gesuiti in the Piazza del Gesú

PLATE 4. Palace near the Piazza della Pace

34

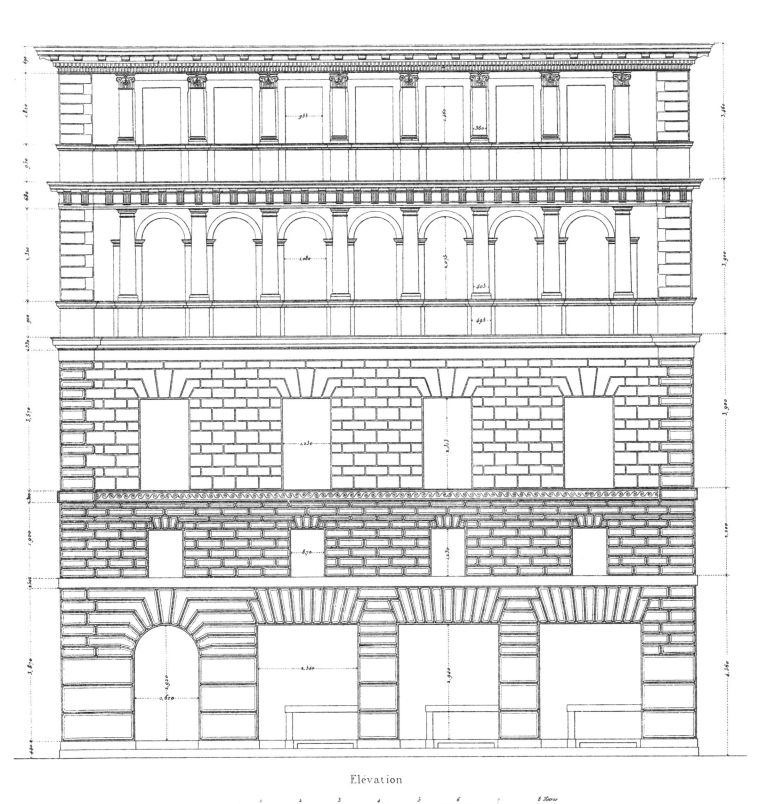

Elévation

8 Metres

Echelle des Elévations

PLATE 5. House on the Via del Governo Vecchio

35

PLATE 6. House on the Piazza Borghese

36

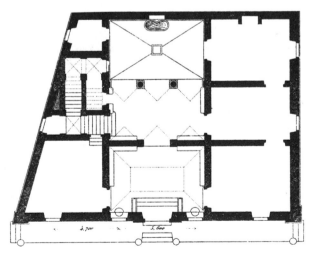

PLATE 7. House on the Via d'Ara Coeli

37

V · THE MASSIMO PALACES

The Pietro Massimo Palace, right, and the Angelo Massimo Palace, left, (plate 1) are masterpieces by Baldassare Peruzzi on the Corso Vittorio Emanuel near the Chancellery Palace. Built for two brothers between 1532 and 1536 they replaced an old family palace destroyed in the Sack of Rome in 1527. The Palazzo Massimo alle Colonne (plate 1), as the first one is often called, was a great model for McKim, Mead & White. Their John Innes Kane house which stood at one time at 610 Fifth Avenue, on what is now part of Rockefeller Center, the University Club on the northwest corner of Fifth Avenue and 54th Street (figs. 1 and 2), both in New York, have many details from it. These details we have illustrated, and I plan to study and make use of them at the earliest opportunity. They seem to have a refinement and, at the same time, strength that I should like to recapture.

What is there that the cicerone can find to say about, for example, the Farnese Hercules? Nothing more than a few words that bear on facts such as where did it stand, who paid for it, who found it, who had owned it. What is there to say about some very dim sarcophagus front of a debased period? When I was doing guide work in Rome I could find a very great deal to say by way of exegesis. Note, for instance, "debased period." That is a value judgment. To Relativists all periods are of equal value. If something is really inept and clumsy and of a low intellectual order, their response is "they meant it to be that way. It expresses its time."

This facade is the only facade in Rome which is completely rusticated, with pilasters on the ground floor, and it is in stucco. The Doric columns and pilasters stretch from one end to the other, contrasting with the severe astylar treatment of the up-per stories with their architrave enframed windows, unadorned balconies and cornice casting a heavy deep shadow (plate 2).

The pilasters have been moved to the ground floor instead of being at the *piano nobile* as the pilasters of the Chancellery nearby, and the rustication is made to climb the height of the building. In addition, the porch columns are themselves arranged in an alternating rhythm so that there are bays with windows in them framed by pilasters in antis to the columns. Above the cornice of the Order is a second band of stone which unites the projecting window sills thus emphasizing the horizontal.

The Doric of the Massimo, observed the French architect, Charles Percier, has the look of true antiquity, which never repeats itself.

The entrance of the loggia of the Massimo is in no way preparation for the upper floors. There is poignant contrast between the deep shadow of the loggia and its Doric cornice and columns and the thinness and flatness of the upper parts. The windows are shallow in relief, with those on the third and fourth floors small and set in scroll frames.

The coupling of columns and the pilasters serves to give the necessary sense of solidity and cohesion to the whole elevation. The extreme projection of the shallow abacus of the Doric columns and pilasters (plate 3) provides an effect of vigor which seems required. The rich moldings which frame the sculpture above the doorway of travertine (plate 4) are of stucco as are the ceiling (plate 5) and the semidomes of the niches at the ends of the porch (plates 4 and 5).

Straighten the porch (plate 5) and you have the porch of the Morgan Library (fig. 3).

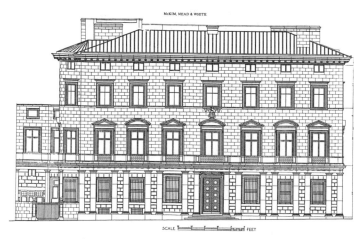

FIG. 1 The John Innes Kane Residence, formerly at 610 Fifth Avenue, New York City, by McKim, Mead & White. From *The Student's Edition of the Monograph of the Work of McKim, Mead & White*

From the portico a hall with a barrel vault leads to the court. The vault is in fresco and stucco relief (plate 6). The court is a Roman atrium and the Roman theme is continued in the atrium and the loggia of the *piano nobile* (plates 7 and 8). The Massimos were open to this influence because they claimed descent from Fabius Maximus Verrucosus. *Cunctator*, or Delayer as he was known, he developed the strategy of delay which eventually led to the defeat of Hannibal and the Carthaginians at the end of the 3rd century B.C. The word Fabian, meaning cautionary, stems from his name. When Camillo Massimo, head of the family around 1800, was asked by Napoleon if it was true about his ancestry, he replied: "I could not prove it. The story has only been told in our family for twelve hundred years."

The ground floor colonnades have pierced vaulting which not only lights the internal loggia but also reduces the discrepancy in height between it and the open loggia of the second floor.

Each of the court elevations (plate 10) offer different treatment with the unity maintained by the superimposed columns, the portico on the entrance side and that of the court end at the bottom of the plate, while that on the left has a wall instead of a loggia on the second floor. Sections of the porticos and loggias (plate 10) give the treatment of the walls and the doorways. The details of the court (plates 10 and 11) are abundant; the entablature of the second story has, for example, a pulvinated frieze enriched with anthemion and acanthus. Inside the hall linking the entrance and the court and

loggias at both ends of the court have elaborate vaults (plate 11). Off one end of the portico on the entrance side of the court (plate 9) a flight of stairs leads to the loggia of the second story (plate 12). Here the ceiling is boldly coffered in hexagons.

The door of the loggia is the entrance to the grand salon (plate 13), the throne room of the palace. Ionic pilasters support a minor cornice with a frieze above part of a major cornice. The large panels of the attic, which is the happiest part of the decoration, represent scenes in the life of the famous Fabius Maximus, while the intermediate panels and sculpture are mythological. The baldachino is an indication of the family's rank. Details of the ceiling and the attic (plate 14) tell of the extraordinary flood of ornament that occurred with the "discovery" of the wonders of the Antique ruins of Rome.

By way of contrast several plates of the Angelo Massimo Palace are also presented. Simpler in many ways than its neighbor next door it shows Baldassare Peruzzi equally at home. The ornament of the facade (plate 15), a longitudinal section and views of two opposite sides of the court (plate 16), a view of the court from the portico on the entrance side and the niches at the far end of the court along with details of the court (plate 17) serve to close the chapter.

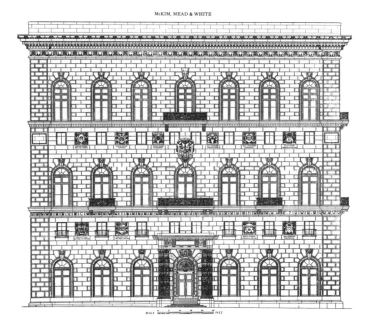

FIG. 2 The University Club, 1 West 54 Street, New York City, 1889–1893, by McKim, Mead & White. From *The Student's Edition of the Monograph of the Work of McKim, Mead & White*

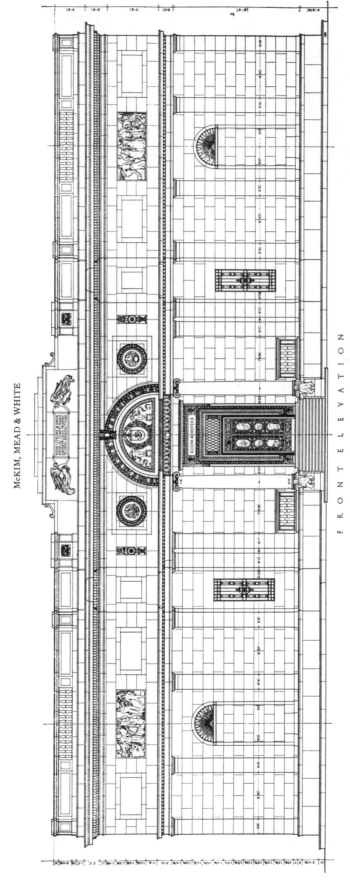

McKIM, MEAD & WHITE

F R O N T   E L E V A T I O N

Fig. 3 The Morgan Library, 29 East 36 Street, New York City, 1902–1907 by McKim, Mead & White. From *The Student's Edition of the Monograph of the Work of McKim, Mead & White*

Vue extérieure des deux Palais et des habitations voisines, prise de la rue di S. Pantaleo.

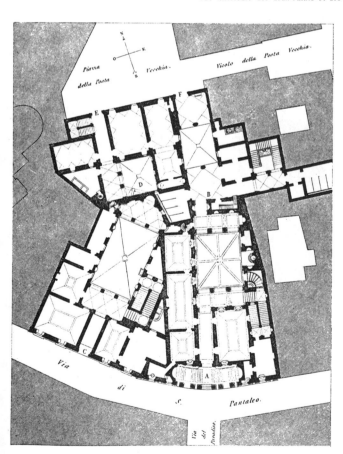

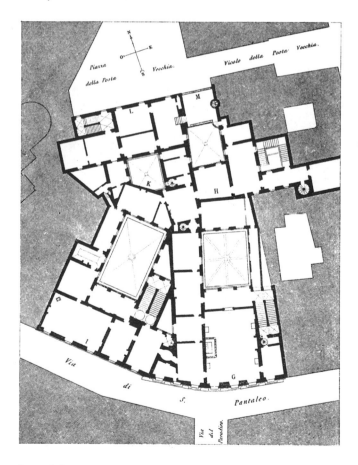

Plan du Rez-de-chaussée des deux Palais.

Plan du Premier Etage des deux Palais.

PLATE 1. The Angelo and Pietro Massimo Palaces with Plans of the Ground and Second Floors

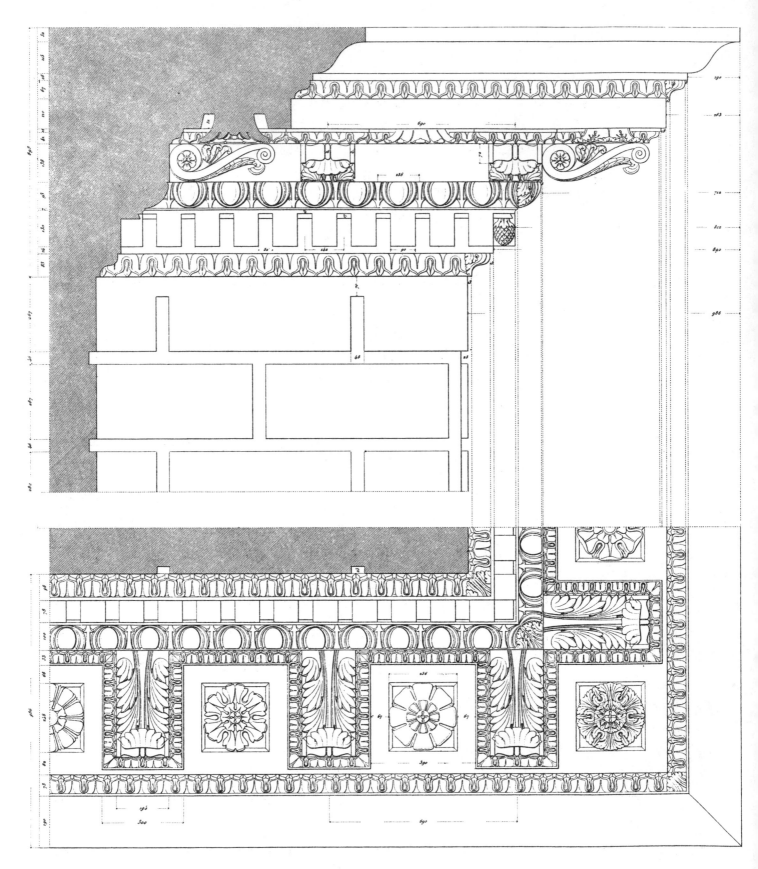

PLATE 2. Cornice of the Pietro Massimo Palace

42

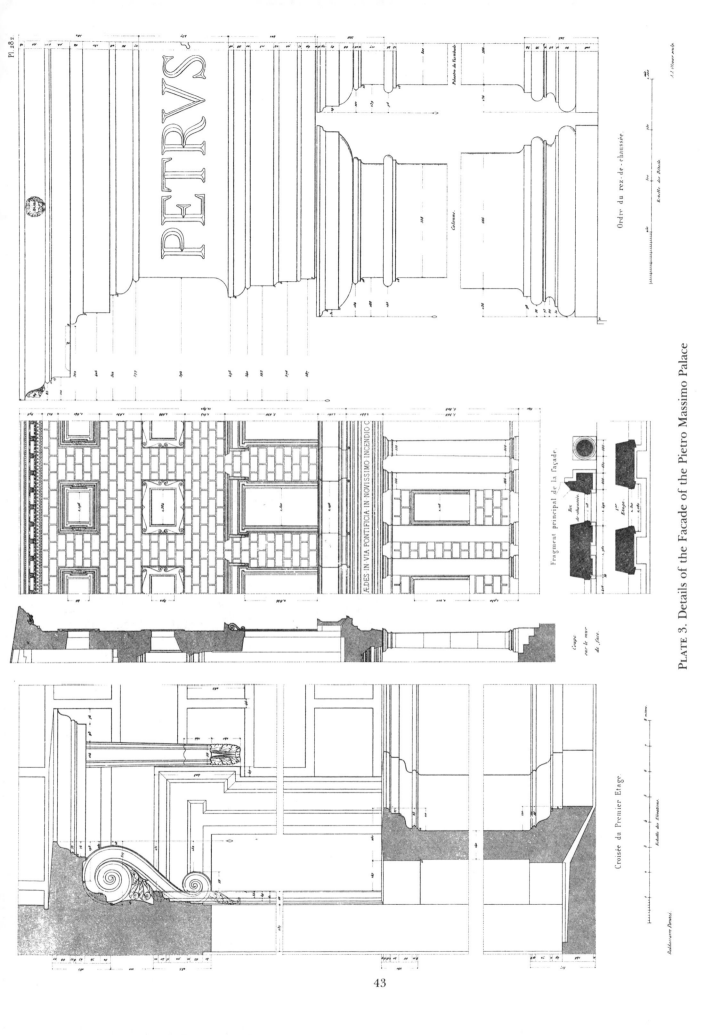

PETRVS

Pl. 282

Ordre du rez-de-chaussée.

Colonne.

Pilastre du Vestibule.

Echelle des Détails.

Fragment principal de la façade.

Rez de-chaussée.

1.er Etage.

...DES IN VIA PONTIFICIA IN NOVISSIMO INCENDIO C

Coupe sur le mur de face.

Croisée du Premier Etage

Echelle des Elévations.

Baldassare Peruzzi.

Plate 3. Details of the Facade of the Pietro Massimo Palace

43

Profil intérieur de la Porte.

Face de la porte d'entrée et soffite de la corniche.

Profil extérieur de la Porte.

Face et profil du banc.

Profil de la grande niche.

Face de la grande niche.

Face, profil et appui de la croisée.

Echelle des Détails.

PLATE 4. Details of the Doorway and of the Niches to Be Found at Either End of the Porch of the Pietro Massimo Palace

44

PLATE 5. Inside the Entrance Porch of the Pietro Massimo Palace

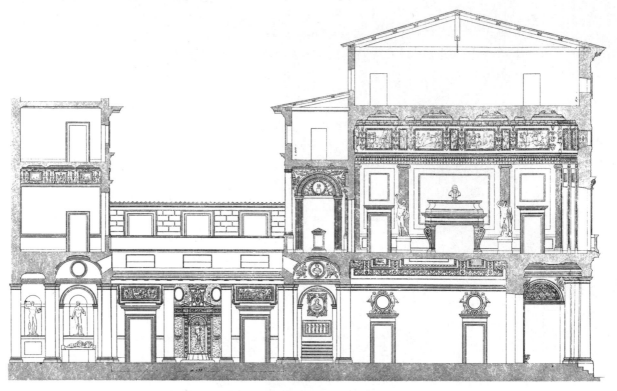

Coupe générale sur le Vestibule, le passage, les deux Portiques et la Cour.

J.J.Olivier et Ribault sculp.

Coupe prise
sur la ligne A B du plan
ci-contre.

PLATE 6. Cross-section showing the Entrance Porch, the Hall, the two Porticos and the Court and the Hall
Leading from the Entrance to the Main Court of the Pietro Massimo Palace

PLATE 7. View of the Court of the Pietro Massimo Palace

Façade latérale à gauche dans la cour.

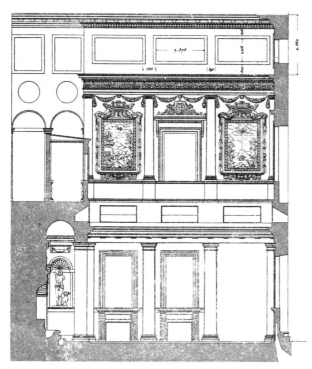

Façade du côté de l'Entrée.

Façade du fond de la cour.

PLATE 8. Court elevations of the Pietro Massimo Palace

48

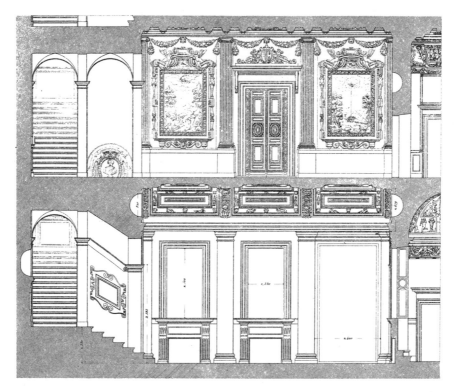

Coupe sur la longueur du Portique, la loge du Premier Etage et l'Escalier.

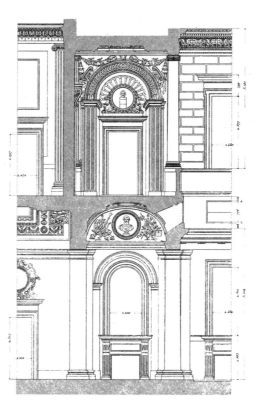

Coupe sur le Portique et la loge du 1ᵉʳ Etage, face du côté de l'Escalier.

Coupe sur le Portique et la loge du 1ᵉʳ Etage, face opposée à l'Escalier.

PLATE 9. Sections of the Court Porticos and Loggias of the Pietro Massimo Palace

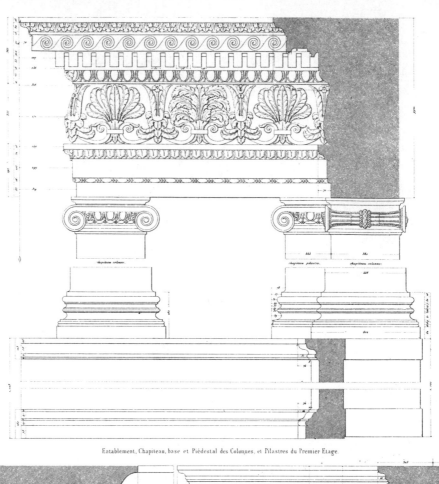

Entablement, Chapiteau, base et Piédestal des Colonnes, et Pilastres du Premier Etage.

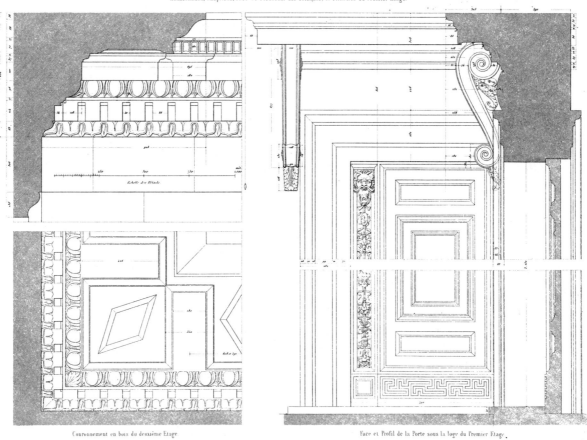

Couronnement en bois du deuxième Etage.

Face et Profil de la Porte sous la loge du Premier Etage.

PLATE 10. Details of the Court of the Pietro Massimo Palace

Détail de la Voûte du Passage situé entre le Vestibule et la cour.

Ensemble de la Voûte ci-dessus.

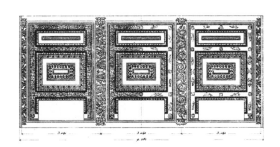

Ensemble des deux Voûtes ci-dessous.

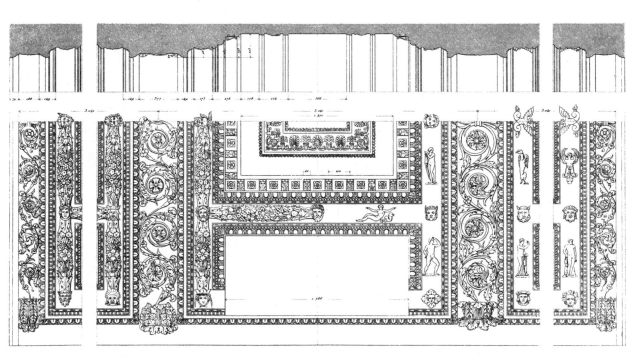

Détail de la Voûte du Portique du fond de la cour.

Détail de la Voûte du Portique de l'Entrée de la cour.

PLATE 11. Details of the Vaulting of the Ground Floor Porticos of the Pietro Massimo Palace

Vue de la Loge du Premier Etage prise en face de l'Escalier.

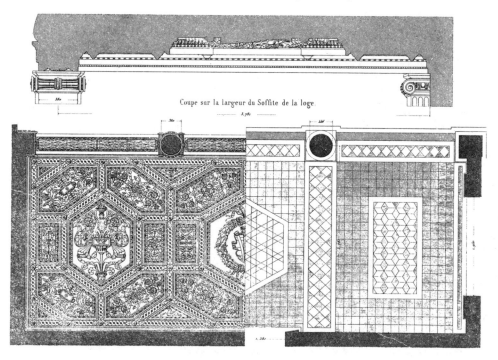

Coupe sur la largeur du Soffite de la loge.

Soffite et Carrelage de la loge du Premier Etage.

PLATE 12. The Loggia of the Second Story or *Piano Nobile* on the Court of the Pietro Massimo Palace

PLATE 13. The Grand Salon of the Second Story of the Pietro Massimo Palace

Detail des Portes latérales.

Variante des Rosaces du Plafond

Variante des Rosaces du Plafond

Détail de   la cheminée.

PLATE 14. Details of the Ceiling and the Frieze of the Grand Salon of the Pietro Massimo Palace

54

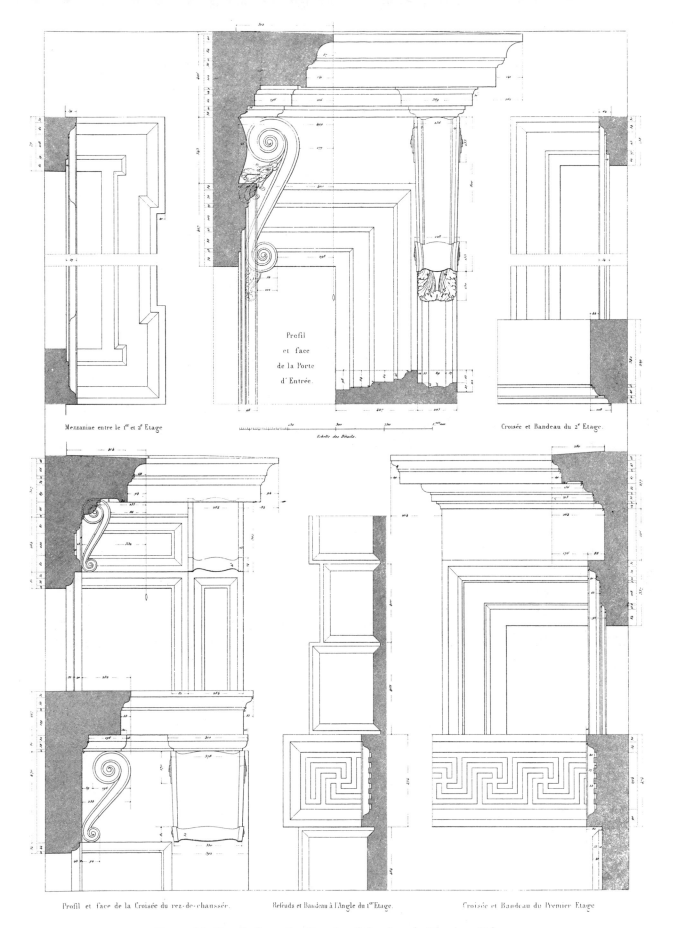

Profil
et face
de la Porte
d´Entrée.

Mezzanine entre le 1ᵉʳ et 2ᵉ Etage

Echelle des Détails.

Croisée et Bandeau du 2ᵉ Etage.

Profil et face de la Croisée du rez-de-chaussée.　　Refends et Bandeau à l'Angle du 1ᵉʳEtage.　　Croisée et Bandeau du Premier Etage.

PLATE 15. Details from the Facade of the Angelo Massimo Palace

Coupe générale sur la longueur.

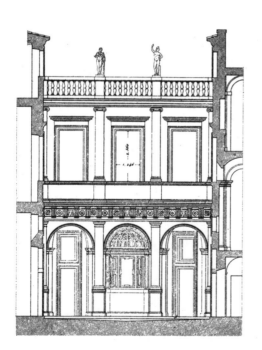

Elévation de la cour, côté du fond.

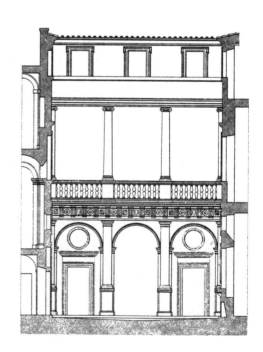

Elévation de la cour, côté de l'Entrée.

PLATE 16. View of the Court Elevations of the Angelo Massimo Palace

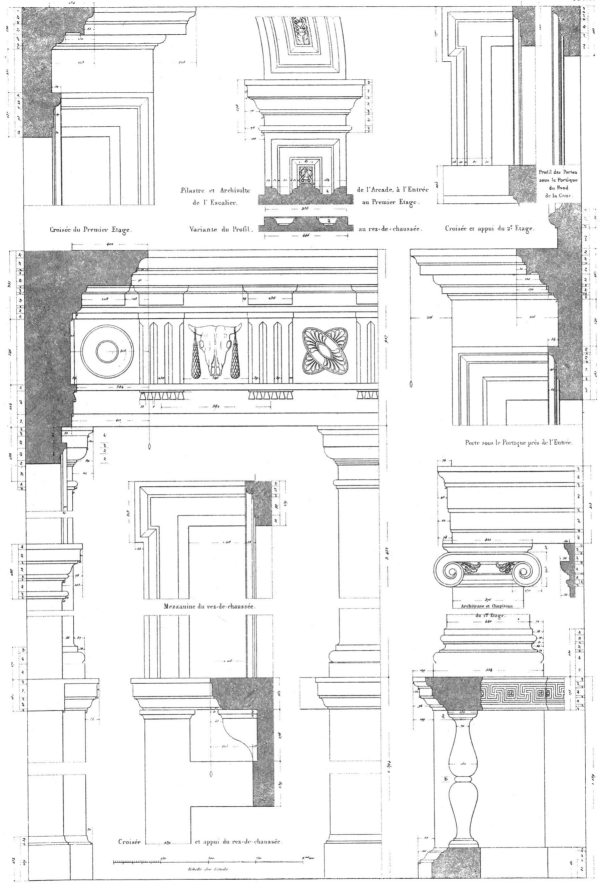

Pilastre et Archivolte
de l'Escalier.

de l'Arcade, à l'Entrée
au Premier Etage.

Profil des Portes
sous le Portique
du Fond
de la Cour.

Croisée du Premier Etage.

Variante du Profil.

au rez-de-chaussée.

Croisée et appui du 2.ᵉ Etage.

Porte sous le Portique près de l'Entrée.

Mezzanine du rez-de-chaussée.

Architrave et Chapiteau
du 1.ᵉʳ Etage.

Croisée et appui du rez-de-chaussée.

Echelle des Détails.

Entablement, Pilastre et Piédestal de l'Ordre; Imposte et Archivolte du rez-de-chaussée.

Base des colonnes, Piédestal et balustre du 1.ᵉʳ Etage.

PLATE 17. Details of the Court Facades of the Angelo Massimo Palace

VI · THE FARNESE PALACE

Roman palaces were more than a pleasant place to live in, and more than a memorial to their builders. They were the capitols of families, and the repositories of their traditions.

The Farnese (plate 1) was the first in the long line of Papal palaces. It is a version of the Florentine palace type, but the sheer mass of the facade and the black tunnel of the entrance have a Roman quality. It is the most monumental of Roman palaces and epitomizes the Grand Manner. "The original lucidity of the idea," wrote Henry James of the Farnese, "its original insolence, one might almost say, triumphs, it keeps the place, always, as great when you see it as when you saw it last, it faces, as so many of the Roman monuments of the first order do, with the assurance of some great natural fact. It brings you round, in especial, to the conviction that, taking one for another, it may rank as the first of its company."

It is an isolated block 250 feet deep and 185 feet wide. The ground floor forms the base of the two floors above which are of equal importance and greater height, the three being respectively 26 feet and 5 inches, 30 feet and 6 inches, and 35 feet and 2 inches. The court is 90 feet square.

The facades are of Roman brick, 1½ inches by 12 inches by 24 inches and pale orange to biscuit in color. The travertine for the dressings came from the quarries at Tivoli outside of Rome, still the principal source of the stone, and not, as is often assumed, from the Colosseum.

The facades have strongly emphasized quoins, the dressed stones at the corners of buildings, but no Florentine rustication or Roman pilasters. The ground floor windows (plates 2 and 3), are provided with straight cornices. Those on the *piano nobile,* or second floor (plates 2 and 3), with alternat-

ing triangular and segmental, that is, part of a circle smaller then a semicircle, pediments in the manner being invented by Raphael. The pediments are supported by columns. The motif is called an *aedicule* or, a shrine framed by two columns supporting an entablature and a pediment. This ancient motif was re-established by Raphael. The aedicules are set upon pedestals connected by string courses, a continuous projecting horizontal band set in the surface of the wall. The aedicules and the pedestals are carried on a belt course—like a string course but heavier—richly decorated. It is these belt courses (fig. 1) that give to the palace its horizontal trinitarian unity.

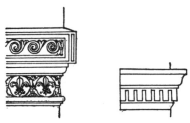

FIG. 1 Belt-courses from the Farnese Palace by Antonio Sangallo the Younger. From William R. Ware, *The American Vignola*

The palace was begun in 1517 by Cardinal Alexander Farnese with Antonio Sangallo the Younger as architect. In 1534 Cardinal Farnese became Pope Paul III. He had Sangallo enlarge the court from three to five bays, and the facade from eleven to thirteen bays. Shops on the street floor were given up, and the narrow entrance transformed into a colonnaded atrium.

In 1546 Sangallo died, and Michelangelo succeeded him. This design mixed elements of the Doric, Ionic and Corinthian Orders, and ignored the Vitruvian rules cherished by Sangallo and Vignola. It is allied to the wall by a frieze with alternating Farnese lilies and acanthus tufts in relief (plate 4). This frieze supplements the cornice in such a way that it enables it to be smaller and have less projection than otherwise. It projects 5 feet 2 inches whereas the cornice of the Strozzi palace in Florence for an equivalant effect projects 7 feet 4 inches. A wood cornice was put on a corner of the palace to judge its effect. The Pope was satisfied and appointed Michelangelo the architect of the palace. The rear of the palace had just been begun, and a few rooms on the *piano nobile* had been built. (The entablature inspired that of the Metropolitan Club by McKim, Mead & White as shown on fig. 2.)

Michelangelo did the cornice, the third floor window enframements, the Farnese coat of arms, the middle part of the piano nobile with the balcony and portal, and the third floor of the court. On the exterior facades he increased the height of the third floor to dramatize the cornice, and because of his fondness for heavy things the top, and

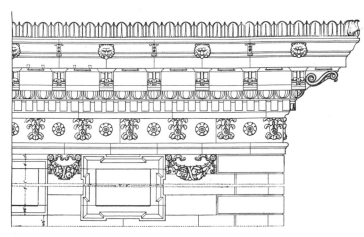

FIG. 2 The entablature of the Metropolitan Club, 1 East 60 Street, New York City, 1891–1894, by McKim, Mead & White. From *The Student's Edition of the Monograph of the Work of McKim, Mead & White*

solid masses over the voids, in this case the windows.

The round-headed windows of the third floor—

FIG. 3 The armorial bearings of the Farnese by Michelangelo. Photo Alinari/Art Resource, Inc.

second floor in Italy—(plate 5) have columns perched on paired consoles. The bottom member of a pediment is the entablature. The entablature has been eliminated except for its corona. You will remember that this is the vertical faced projection in the upper part of a cornice, above the bed mold and below the cymatium. The corona bears the split fillet. This fillet, a flat-faced projection, goes all around the triangle of the pediment on one plane (plate 5). The cymatium goes above it on the raking cornices of the gable. In Michelangelo's enframement the *extrados*, the upper surface of an arch of the molding that frames the window opening just touches, just kisses, the underside of the horizontal cornice. No one has ever done this before or since. Anyone else would have left a decent interval—a margin for error—between the arch and the corona.

Michelangelo gave *chiaroscuro*, the play of light and shade, to the flatness of Sangallo's facade with the huge armorial bearing (fig. 3) of the Farnese in dramatic relief (omitted from plates 2 and 3) and by deeply recessing the central bay of the *piano nobile*. He framed it with a long flat lintel born at either end by columns of Antique marble, Verde Antico from Thessaly. Flat lintels are a favorite motif of Michelangelo's and they are a denial of rational construction; large, hard to move, easily cracked monoliths are not the best way to span an opening. You know that there must be relieving arches concealed behind them. We have met these lintels at the Campidoglio.

Over the entrance to the 'tunnel' entrance there is a wide cornice, and on this he put a balustrade with pedestals (fig. 3).

The beau ideal of the Renaissance man is Leon Battista Alberti, a gentleman, revering Antiquity, Vitruvius and good architectural 'practice,' humanist, even neo-pagan. About one hundred years later Michelangelo is the complete opposite. He denies rational construction; he dismembers the Orders; he rough-handles the classical vocabulary. Yet the strangeness of his work touches the thoughts of hearts. Francis Bacon wrote, "There is no excellent beauty that hath not some strangeness in the proportions." Classical Architecture might be compared to the sea, sometimes it is calm and blue with placid wavelets, sometimes it is dark and storm-wracked with mountainous combers and the *terribilità*, a word applied to any art of austere and tragic grandeur of the Master.

The court has the cloistered ground floor of all palaces, but now in accordance with the Bramante tradition it is based on the Colosseum and the Theatre of Marcellus (see Ch. III, *Courtyards*, figs. 1 and 2) with columns set against piers rather then the light Florentine columns and arches of the Cancelleria.

When the palace was augmented in 1541 the height of the ground floor arcades had to be increased. To do this the impost blocks, the molded member on which an arch rests, were doubled (fig. 4). This was a step with no precedent and, as far as I know, has never been done again and, yet, as we can see from plate 6 the result is austere and splendid.

FIG. 4 The double impost of the ground floor arcades in the court of the Farnese. From William R. Ware, *The American Vignola.*

The *piano nobile* or second floor, as designed by Sangallo, (plate 6) has no gallery but noble pedimented windows set into blank arcades and an Ionic Order. This was left unaltered by Michelangelo except that the entablature was heightened and decorated by a frieze with garlands and masks alternating with the Farnese lily (plates 7 and 8).

The segmented window pediments of the third story (plate 7) have the usual cornice beneath them, and at each end a block that stops midway down the frieze and is unsupported. The block's width is taken up again in the tympanum, the vertical recessed part of a pediment. Each of these tympanum blocks has a ring at its outer edge, and from

FIG. 5 The third-story window of the courtyard facade of the Farnese Palace by Michelangelo. Photo John Barrington Bayley

Fig. 6 View of the topmost cornice of the courtyard of the Farnese Palace by Michelangelo. Photo Courtesy Istituto Centrale per il Catalogo e la Documentazione

these are suspended garlands that go to an ox scull in the center. Over the forehead and horns of the skull hangs a string of husks.

A plain band of stone goes over the window (fig. 5 and plate 9) and goes down the sides to stop at a console, an ornamented bracket with a compound curve outline, but the console does not carry anything. The rounded part of the console on top has a fish-scale pattern, and the rest is a triglipyh, customarily one of a number of blocks with vertical grooves separating the metopes in a Doric frieze. From this a pendent panel hangs below the window sill emphasizing verticality. At the very bottom of the panel there is a circular motif that looks like a doorbell.

The Corinthian capitals of the pilasters have plain acanthus leaves although this is about as far as you can go with acanthus leaves in travertine, a deeply pitted stone.

You will have noticed small rectangular panels let into the dado which runs on top of the cornice of the *piano nobile* that serves as base for the top story pilasters (plate 7). Some of these panels are blind, but some are glazed, they are the windows of an entresol, a low story between two higher ones. It must not be supposed, looking at a Roman palace, that all those tall windows give onto rooms of the same height. In the Farnese, there are many hideaway rooms reached by small staircases, often circular.

One principal room, the *Salle des Gardes* or the

Hall of Hercules, boasts of two sets of five windows facing the square, one row at the piano nobile and a second at the top floor, with an equivalent two sets of three looking out on the side street. This enormous room is 67 feet by 47 feet and 59 feet high.

The cornice of the court (fig. 6 and plate 9) is a strange amalgam of a *cavetto cymatium* on top of a corona, but instead of being vertical it slopes outward from the top to the bottom at an angle of about fifteen degrees. A bed mold carries a corona which has *guttae* hanging free with no taenia, an egg-and-dart beneath, no frieze and an architrave with small masks of bearded and crowned men set at close intervals.

The cornice dissolves when seen from below, and it was not meant to be seen in conjunction with the other stories. That there is no mismatch between the two manners of design, Sangallo's suave classicism versus the austere discords of Michelangelo's

Fig. 7 The "tunnel" of the Municipal Building, Chambers and Centre Street, New York City, 1907–1916, by McKim, Mead & White. Photo Dick Schuler

genius, is due to the use of the same travertine and the lapse of the centuries.

The Piazza Farnese (plate 1) in front of the palace is 260 feet wide and 160 feet from the front of the palace to the other side. Via dei Baullari comes straight into the middle of the other side, and the axis runs straight to the entrance, the "tunnel," of the palace. This is a unique condition in Rome which is a medieval congeries of streets and alleys with nothing at right angles or on axis. Flanking the axis in the piazza are fountains with the lily of the Farnese at the top, jetting water into enormous tubs. The tubs are in grey Egyptian granite and came from the Baths of Caracalla; the fountains atop the tubs are seventeenth century. In the time of Paul III there were no fountains in the piazza which was used for bull fights and tournaments.

The big rusticated archway on the piazza opens into a passage vestibule (plate 10). The semi-circular vault is supported by columns of polished red Egyptian granite, like those on the porch of the Pantheon. They came from the Forum and were discovered during excavations ordered by Paul III. The passage-vestibule is in effect a small Roman basilica without the apse. The Chambers Street passage (fig. 7) of the City of New York's Municipal Building by William Mitchell Kendall of McKim, Mead & White is a simulacrum of the Farnese "tunnel." The vault is made up of coffers of terra cotta in natural baked clay color and figured with Sangallo's usual virtuoso ornamentation. The aisles have flat ceilings with terra cotta coffers laid between stone beams. The walls have niches between half-columns with benches below them. There are also benches around the base of the palace—a civic benefaction. Since the Antique columns from the Forum were too short Sangallo mounted them on little pedestals. Sangallo must not be underestimated, his solutions are always very tight, and his flair for ornament, as seen in the cedar ceilings (plate 11 and fig. 8) of the palace is unexcelled.

This plate (plate 12) fortunately shows the court as it was first built. On the *piano nobile* there were three open bays on the court. We can see the sky through them in this picture. There were five open bays on the back of the palace looking out over Michelangelo's proposed grand axis. This axis began really in the Campo dei Fiori. From there it went down the Via dei Baullari to the Piazza Farnese. The Via dei Baullari bisects the Piazza Farnese's side opposite the palace and is perpendicular to it. The axis continues across the Piazza, enters the

FIG. 8 Cedar ceiling in a room of the Farnese Palace with the lilies of the Farnese. Photo John Barrington Bayley

'tunnel,' crosses the court, passes between the Farnese Hercules and the Farnese Flora, both now in the National Museum in Naples, in the cloister on the far side, enters the 'tunnel' which was richly embellished with this end in view, bisects the Farnese Bull, now in the same museum, which had been made into a fountain by Michelangelo, travels through the garden to the Tiber, a matter of a hundred yards, and climbs the Janiculum Hill to infinity. In 1598 the five bays facing the Tiber were enclosed to create a gallery. The gallery was frescoed by the Caracci, 1599 to 1604.

The "Flora" and "Hercules" are both about fifteen feet high, and they were found between 1534 and 1549 in the ruins of the Baths of Caracalla. Antique sculpture was and is very much a part of the Roman palace scene. It sets the tone, and these heroic dimensions were built to provide a setting for it. The shining floors and elaborate ceilings, gilded furniture and vases, chandeliers and girandoles, i.e., a branched support for candles often hung with crystals, tapestries and damasks, might seem over-rich without this marble, this silent au-

63

dience of gods and goddesses, legislators in togas, soldiers in armor, bacchic sarchophagi, polychrome busts and heads of emperors, nymphs and satyrs.

The palace had been rented by French ambassadors to the Holy See, on and off, from the middle of the sixteenth century. In 1731 the last Farnese died, and the palace was inherited by Charles III, king of the Two Sicilies, son of Philip V of Spain and Elizabeth Farnese, and its statues and other treasures were removed to Naples.

Rome was a republic under the French in 1798, but the republic fell within a year. What followed, that is, the restoration of papal government, furnished the source for Puccini's opera, *Tosca,* via the French playwright Victorien Sardou. Baron Scarpia, the presumed ruler of Rome, had his headquarters in the palace, as we know from the second act.

During the Napoleonic period the palace was the embassy to the Holy See of Joachim Murat, King of Naples. After the restoration of the Bourbons it served the same purpose until 1864 when the king and queen of Naples took refuge in it after their kingdom had been overthrown by Garibaldi. They lived there until 1870. In 1874 the French foreign office decided to rent the palace for its embassy to the Kingdom of Italy. In 1911 the French offered to buy the palace, and a sale was made with the proviso that the Italian government might redeem it in twenty-five years. In 1936 the Italians did redeem it, and gave the French a ninety-nine year lease for a rent of one lira. According to Georgina Masson this was done in exchange for an equivalent lease on the Hotel Galiffet, the Italian embassy in Paris.

This gallery, The Caracci Gallery (plate 11) ranks with the "Stanze of Raphael" and the Sistine Chapel as the third of the great classical decorations of Rome.

The gallery is 66 feet long and 22 feet wide with a barrel vault. The entrance door is framed in a green marble of an extremely rare kind from the Baths of Queen Zenobia at Bagni. The side walls are divided off with Corinthian pilasters. In between the pilasters are shellcapped niches. The niches now contain copies of ancient statues. In the days of the Farnese they contained Antique vases and bronze statues. Over the niches are shields held up by winged cupids; they are painted with various symbols and allegories. Over these are busts in cir-

cular niches alternating with rectangular pictures in frames with *canephorae,* women carrying baskets on their heads, to either side. At either end of the room are doors, and over them a big picture framed with double *crossettes,* a projection in the casing of a door or window at the junction of a jamb and head (sometimes called Greek Ears) at the corners. The pilasters are set upon a high dado with a Greek fret motif at the top and set with feigned marble panels under the niches.

All the foregoing architecture is in *Bianco Sporco,* or Dirty White, and in *Parcel Gilt.* The latter means that small surfaces are gilt—the moldings of the pilaster panels, the backgrounds of arabesques, the inner shells of the niche hoods, the ribbons of garlands, the leaves of the Corinthian capitals, the decorative bands of honeysuckle flower and leaves on the face of the niches' arches etc. The stucco work here is of extreme richness and the parcel gilding accents and makes it 'read', giving it a magnificent effect. From the baseboard to the cornice we have interior architecture in true relief.

Above the cornice the architectural relief is feigned in paint, or *trompe l'oeil,* an illusion where, in the use of perspective and foreshortening and cast shadows, the eye is deceived into taking that which is painted for that which is real. This is a very ancient kind of painting.

The heroic proportions of Michelangelo's figures are present here, but the Caracci figures are more full-blown, less sculptural and richer in color. *Trompe l'oeil* metal medallions are present in both rooms, gold in the Sistine Chapel and verdigris bronze here. The illusionist architecture is the same color in both rooms, but here the decorative details are far richer—geometric frets, leaves (acanthus, laurel, vine, olive), festoons, swags, ribbons, arabesques, vases, heads.

All the pictures in the gallery have one theme, the triumph of love in the universe, or as it is sometimes put, "The Loves of the Gods." A subtle veil of melancholy seems to lie over all these pictures, almost as if the artists felt regret for the beautiful Antique fables, by this time so far from their own time. However, pathos, or melancholy, is endemic to classical art. You can see it in the Roman portrait busts, (the busts of the stoics), and in the constant references to the brevity of existence in Antique poetry. "Creatures of a day, what is anyone?" (Pindar) is very typical. This melancholy comes from a pre-Christian world-view. Christianity brought hope.

PLATE 1. The Farnese Palace and its Square

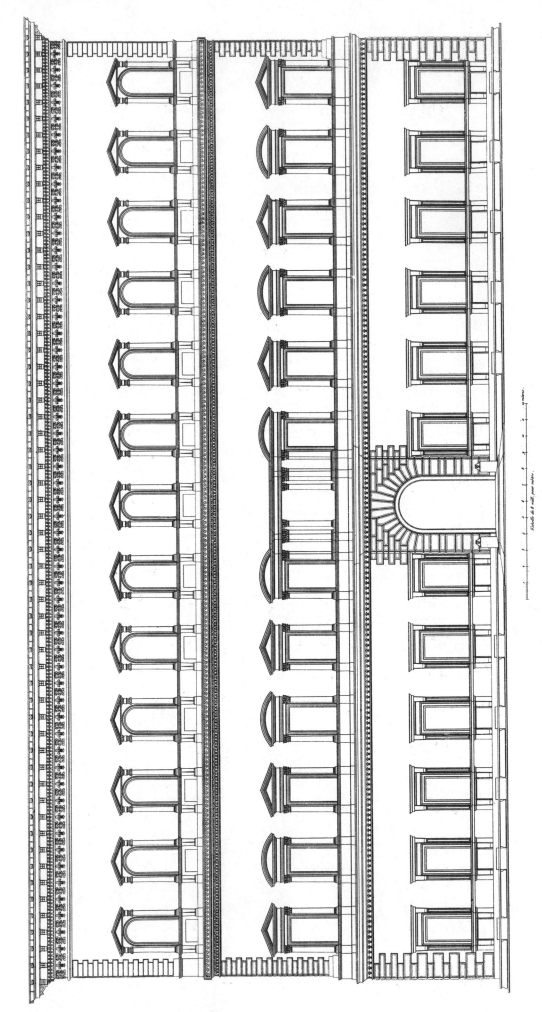

PLATE 2. The Principal Elevation of the Farnese Palace

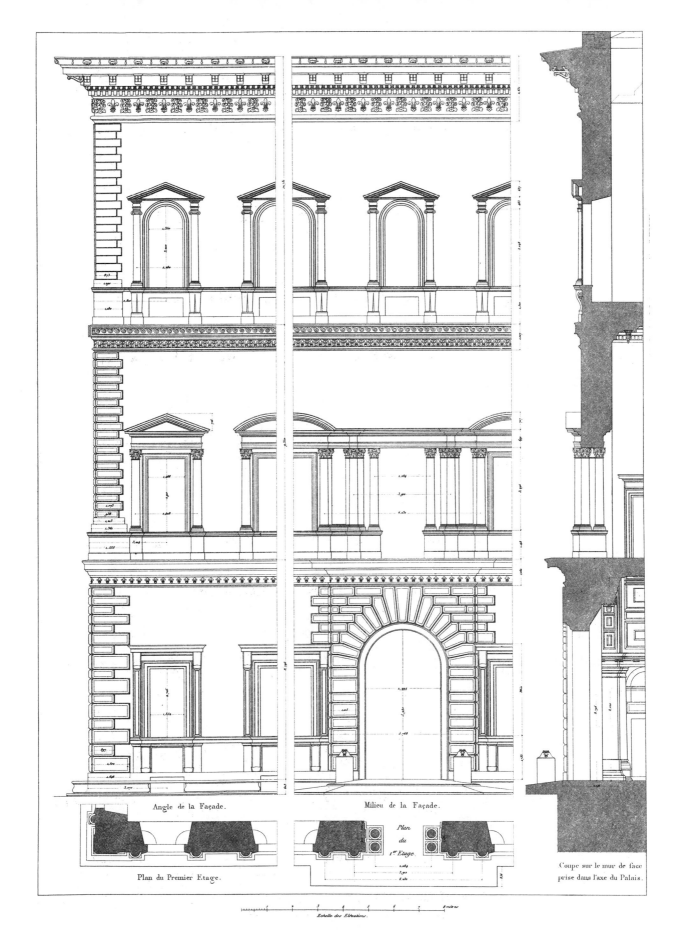

Angle de la Façade.

Milieu de la Façade.

Plan
du
1er Etage.

Plan du Premier Etage.

Coupe sur le mur de face
prise dans l'axe du Palais.

Echelle des Elevations.

PLATE 3. Elements of the Elevations

67

Coupe sur les Soffites entre les modillons.

Coupe sur la face et sur l'axe des fleurs de Lis.

Ci - dessous

Plan des Soffites entre les modillons.

Echelle des détails.

PLATE 4. Details of the Main Cornice of the Facade

68

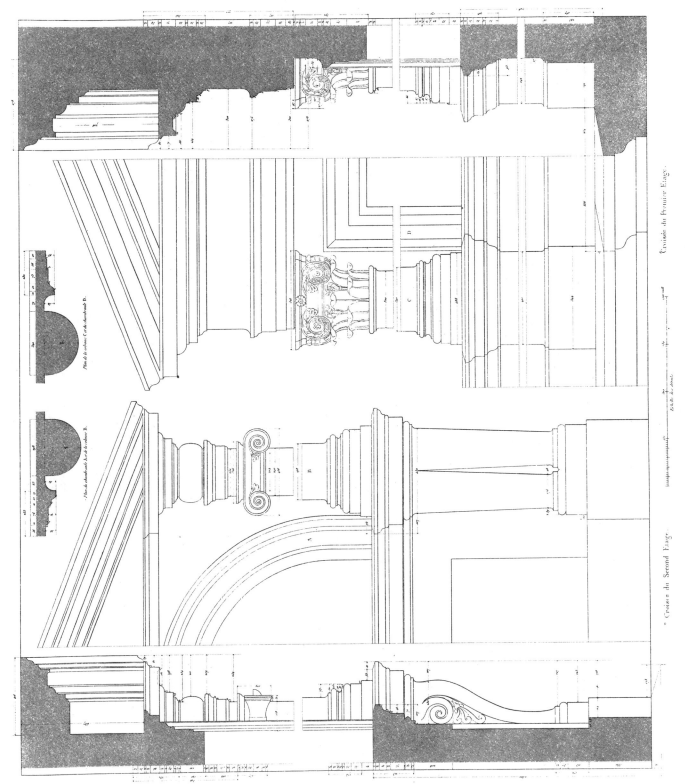

Plan de la colonne C et du chambranle D.

Plan de chambranle A et de la colonne B.

° Croisée du Second Étage.

Croisée du Premier Étage.

Échelle des détails

PLATE 5. Details of the Window Enframements of the Facade

69

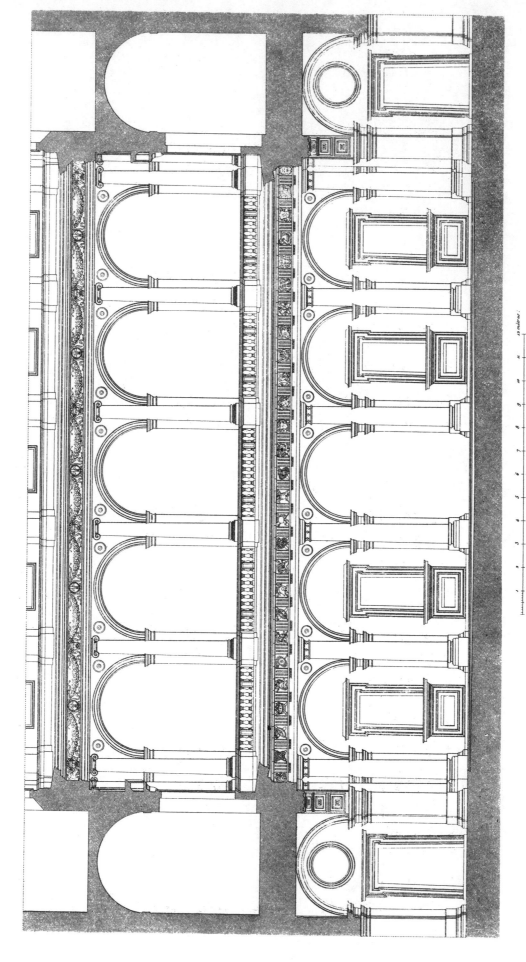

Echelle de 8 mill. pour metre.

Plate 6. The First and Second (*Piano Nobile*) Stories of the Court

70

Entrée du Grand Escalier, Angle et première travée de la cour.

Vestibule du fond de la cour et profil de la façade postérieure.

Echelle des Elévations.

PLATE 7. Main Parts of the Court Facade

Imposte et caissons de l'intrados des arcades.

Rosace entre les archivoltes.

Saillie des pilastres.

Pilastre entre les balustres.

Face des pilastres.

Entablement, chapiteau, base et piédestal
de l'ordre.

Échelle des détails.

Face et saillie des pilastres de l'intérieur
du portique.

PLATE 8. Details of the *Piano Nobile* of the Court with Details of the Portico Pilasters (right)

Face et Profil de la Croisée.   DÉTAILS DU DEUXIÈME ÉTAGE.   Entablement, Chapiteau, b:

ci-dessous

Coupe

sur l'Entablement.

PLATE 9. Details of the Third Story Windows and Details and Profile of the Main Entablature of the Court
Facade

73

PLATE 10. The "Tunnel" or Entrance to the Farnese Palace

Vue de la Galerie f située au premier Etage et peinte par Annibale Caracci.

Echelle des Élévations.

PLATE 11. The Carracci Gallery and the Ceiling of a Salon on the *Piano Nobile*

75

PLATE 12. View of the Court Seen from the Portico near the Entrance

VII · THE DECORATION OF VAULTS

Lest it worry any Rationalists in the crowd, i.e., those who would hold that all forms are structural, and those who believe the vault obsolete since we now use steel, lest they worry about several pages devoted to the decoration of vaults, I would like to point out that, with the possible exception of the grotto entrance to the icehouses (plate 1) of the Villa Giulia or Villa di Papa Giulio, all these vaults are false. They do not carry floors over them. The floors are carried on wooden beams, expensive and troublesome. Steel is far better. The vaults are shells. I was surprised to see in bombed buildings after World War II that some of the vaults of very palatial buildings were of lathe and plaster or even reeds and plaster.

The icehouse is an excellent example of a pilastered room. Here the pilasters are on pedestals. Note the very extensive use of egg-and-dart molding. The form of decoration on the rear wall which suggests the flow of water is called *"congélations."* (The architectural vocabulary flops about between Greek, Latin and French, and when you translate it into English it not only seems flat, but it is also not understood.) The stucco reliefs in the ceiling are based on some Antique remains. Stucco work of this kind is made from wooden molds which are often kept in stock by the *stuccatori* or stucco workers.

The vault of the portico of the Villa courtyard (plate 2) with cupids and birds playing and flying in a grape arbor is archetypal and goes back to antiquity. It has been used over and over again. The portico is part of the grand court of the Villa.

The loggia of Cupid and Psyche in the Villa Farnesina (plate 3), which is directly acoss from the Farnese Palace, originally served as entrance vestibule. In painting it, Raphael was assisted by Giulio Romano, Francesco Penni and Giovanni da Udine. We do not have here the recreation of a Roman room as in one of the great ancient baths but the decoration of a Renaissance loggia with a ceiling which does not reflect the divisions of an ancient vault but the spandrels and lunettes on a Renaissance vault, all punctuated by the dazzling rich festoons of flowers and fruit painted by Udine. One of the most famous rooms in history, it is like a mythological pagan counterpart in a minor mode of the Biblical and sacred vault of the Sistine Chapel.

The house was planned as a Renaissance recreation of a Roman villa. In it were frescoes based on Lucian, Ovid, Virgil and Apuleius (as here). The frescoes have been much damaged by the atmosphere and by restoration. It is hard to imagine how they must have looked before the openings to the left were filled with glass. The narrative is incomplete and was perhaps to have been finished with tapestries on the flat walls. The lunettes were actually painted in false windows. Letarouilly has filled them with figure completions of his own. This room is to inspire you, readers, as an example of what a great room in decoration and in size and proportion can be.

This room (plate 4) in the Palazzo di Firenze, today the seat of the *Società Nazionale Dante Alighieri*, has a floor of ceramic tile interlaced with bands of travertine, travertine walls, and a ceiling in colors more restricted than they would be indoors. The garden side is now glazed.

A section (plate 5) of the same palace is a small room facing the garden. Its vaulting (plate 6) has designs of stucco or paint, or, best, a combination of both.

Visitors to Rome often complain that they have stiff necks. "Oh, if they'd only put all these pictures on the walls!" It is different when you live there. Sitting down makes things easier. Lying down is best of all, and many of the rooms around town that are now furnished as salons were originally bedrooms.

A ceiling is the largest uninterrupted surface in any room, and presently the greatest of all opportunities for decoration.

PLATE 1. The Grotto Leading to the Entrance of the Icehouse of the Villa Giulia built by Pope Julius III (Cocchi del Monte).

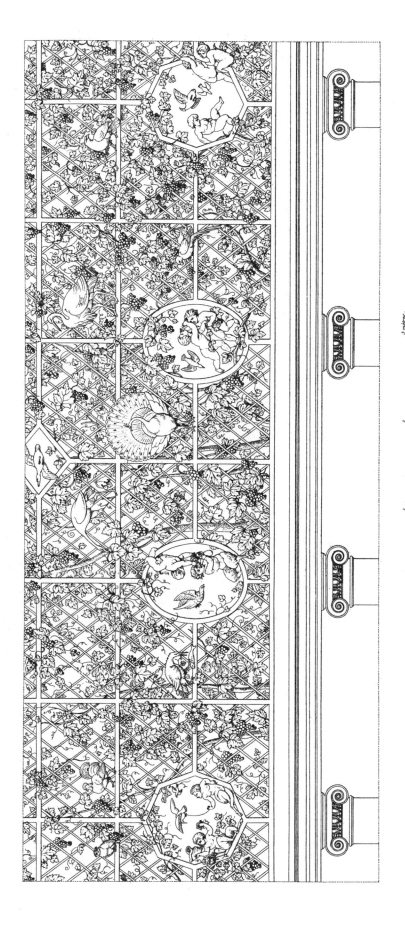

Ⅰ PLATE 2. The Vault of the Portico of the Courtyard of the Grand Court of the Villa Giulia

79

PLATE 3. The Loggia of Cupid and Psyche in the Villa Farnesina

PLATE 4. The Garden Loggia of the Palace of Florence or Palazzo di Firenze

81

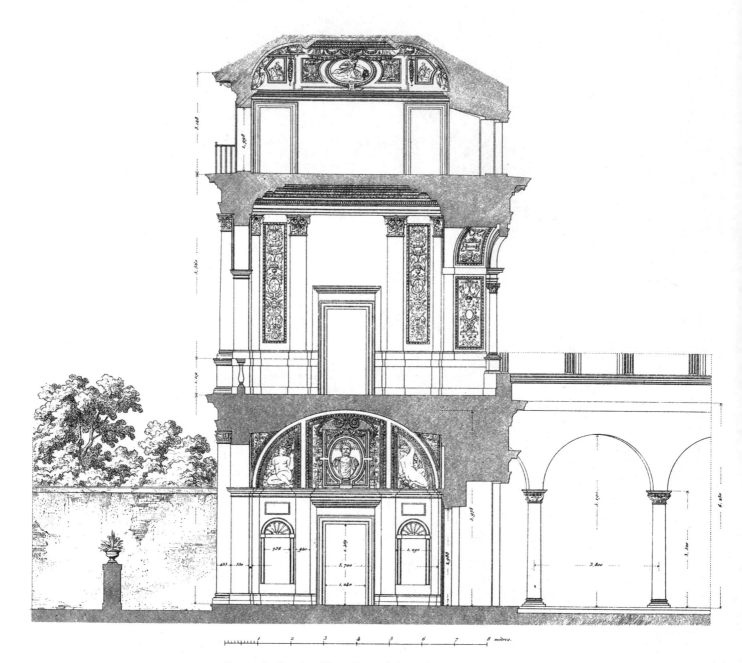

PLATE 5. Section Elevation of the Palace of Florence

PLATE 6. Vault of the Small Room on the Ground Floor of the Palace of Florence

VIII · VILLAS

We have met with the Villa Giulia or the Villa di Papa Giulio (plate 1) in the chapter on vaults. It was Vignola's first Roman building. As it now survives it is the nucleus of what was formerly a much more extensive scheme. The plan (plate 2) shows a straight front with the entrance leading to a semicircular portico (plates 3 and 4), a grand cortile with a formal garden, a sunken court embraced by summer rooms, approached by sweeping flights of steps and having a central fountain grotto with caryatic figures, rippling water and tiny cascades. A further garden lay beyond.

Here a series of courtyards and their connecting passageways (plate 5) are placed on the central axis but the entrance doors linking them are obscured and in the first courtyard, other possible exits are made to seem more "natural" ways of leaving it. But only if one discovers or is guided to the passageway on the axis can one enter the fountain beyond. On entering, the visitor was abruptly transported from the broad surface of the first courtyard to the top of a crescent stairway that led into a deep well (plates 5 and 6). Within its richly decorated walls, he was surrounded by works of sculpture, flowers, birds and fountains which he was free to explore down to another level. If he persisted he would discover hidden here on the left a small spiral stairway that led to the last court, an enclosed garden. (Today the stairway is barred; access to the garden is from the ground level.)

At the Villa Giulia surprise after surprise is encountered within a small compass as hemicycles and nymphaea reveal themselves as though designed expressly for evening parties and theatricals.

Part of the setting is a grotto (plates 6 and 7), a revived Renaissance form of the classical nymphaeum, originally a natural rocky cave, fern grown, over which water dripped, or deep alcove below the gnarled roots of a tree, moss-grown and sacred to a nymph. Strangest of all grottoes were those where the Orades or mountain nymphs lived. The local tufa, a volcanic rock, was especially good for holding dripping fern. The nymphaeum at the villa was the work of Vasari, disciple of Michelangelo.

The water originally came from the Aqua Vergine, whose ancient aqueduct Julius III had restored. It now comes from the Acqua Marcia.

The best known aspect of the Villa Giulia is, of course, the facade (plate 1), always mentioned with the name of Vignola. Its center was an innovation. Its bays are designed in the guise of a triumphal arch and are executed in freestone. It is the only entrance that is a walled enclosure.

The casino of the Villa Giustiniani/Massimo (plate 8) refers to the dwelling, the villa to the whole property. (The property, it might be added, has long since been devoured, lately by apartment houses and a school.) The interior here is known for its frescoes executed in 1818–1829 by a group of German artists called the Nazarenes with subjects such as "Milton Visiting Galileo," "Christians under the Saracen Yoke," the style being based on painters before Raphael.

To have an idea of Roman scale, notice the entrance door; it is probably about eight feet high. On the ground floor the windows are high in the wall and are meant to light the rooms rather than to be looked out of. On the second floor the windows are lower, and one would have looked out of them over the gardens, and parterres which actually only 'read' when seen from above.

The windows had casements set with leaded glass. It is very easy to reproduce these as there are many documents showing feigned windows that were painted on walls to balance schemes of interior decoration at the Villa Farnesina.

The outside is decorated with busts on rondels, sarcophagus fronts under the second floor windows, and Antique reliefs over the ground floor windows and between the sarcophagus fronts.

The view we have shows the back of the villa, the garden front. Looking at the plan we should remember that Italian houses do not have closets. The high ceilings would make the upper part of a closet inaccessible. Instead we have wardrobes (*armadio*). They are eminently practical because all the space in them is readily reached, and their panels can be used for arabesques. Perhaps some inventive person will devise bathtubs and basins for them; toilets go in wall thicknesses. Adapting Italian residential plans to our use—we require bathrooms—is a grave problem for the designer. So far most designers have tried to poke them in, but as soon as that is done the clarity, the simplicity, of the originals is lost. The result is that the bulk, the cubic footage, of the house is devoured by closets, service stairs, and hallways, and a big house finds itself with no big rooms or panache. The proper way to handle the problem is the way it has always been done. The next time you are in the Farnese Palace notice that, in the Salle des Gardes (fig. 1), the windows are so fixed in the wall that there are two steps and even two seats contained within the thickness of the wall. This means a reveal of four feet or so. In the Pitti Palace in Florence, on the ground floor, there is a reveal of at least eight feet and it contains a little flight of steps, say seven or eight risers needed to look out the window. (A reveal is that part of a jamb which lies between the window and inner surface of the wall, and it is cut in plan on the diagonal, and this is called a splay.) With our modern techniques, and although art and morals do not progress, there is such a thing as *material progress*. We should be able to construct toilets within the thicknesses or, better, feigned thickness of the walls, to be reached from a concealed door. It means a door which is not architecturally expressed with an enframement, a door case, and panelling. Rather it makes itself part of the wall: it carries the baseboard of the room and the dado, and is covered with cloth or paper or paint like the rest of the wall. I might add that over the centuries special hardware has been developed for these doors, and they have always given, and do give, trouble. Circumstances of great distinction are not always comfortable. I demand comfort as much as the next man, but if comfort is all you demand, then I think you had better stick to a ranch house and saying your prayers in bed.

In figure 2 you will see the plans for the Dinsha house (1973). You will see the plans of the rooms, except those in the service wing on the right hand side, are surrounded by heavy "poché." This is a French word meaning to give someone a black eye. It also has another meaning and the word was in constant use at the Ecole des Beaux Arts and in all the architectural schools because if you draw two lines in ink then you can run a wash of ink between them, and they hold it in place. This is the basis of Beaux Arts planning. You surround your rooms with adequate "poché," and it is understood that structure, mechanical plans, and the general prose of architecture, is included in the "poché." (How we laughed at this in Bauhaus days, we were going to *express* all those things, not that we or our professors knew anything about them.) "Poché" came to mean not only ink, the purest and blackest Chinese, but also just darkening in service areas to allow the essential spaces to "read,' as you see in the Dinsha plan. You will observe that all the win-

FIG. 1 A corner of the *Salle des Gardes* of the Farnese Palace, showing the deep reveals of the windows. Photo John Barrington Bayley

FIG. 2. Elevations and plan of the Edward Dinsha house by John Barrington Bayley

dows of the principal rooms have enormously deep reveals, or splays. They give room for shutters, and for an infinity of closets, but first-off they are their own reward because they light the rooms. The sunlight reflects off of them, and there are no curtains next to the glass. The deep splay gives a great feeling of protection and of well-being, probably, it suggests that the walls are immensely thick. In "doublure" we lie to tell a greater truth (see p. 115).

The Villa Farnesina stand on the right bank of the Tiber across from the Farnese Palace. Here is a plan (plate 9) of the original entrance front, today the garden front. The famous loggia with Raphael's mural of Cupid and Psyche (plate 10) is behind the five high-arched bays of which only three are visible here.

The two sides of the exterior appear to be those of a two-storied palace. The articulation of these "urban facades" with Doric pilasters and oblong windows was an innovation in Rome. The Chancellery and its kin had round-headed windows on the ground floor and the *piano nobile* above. There is no marble incrustation and no rhythmic pilaster grouping. The square windows over the ground floor show that there is an entresol or *piano ammezzato,* a low ceiling utility floor between the ground floor and the *piano nobile.* We can see the same kind of windows in the deep ornamental frieze of the cornice, a device with Rosellino of Siena.

Today the five bays are glazed so that the contrast of void and solid has been done away with. The facade also was originally decorated with frescoes which have long since weathered away, and today we have the contrast between the bare walls and the richness of the frieze.

This entrance, now the garden front with its flanking wings, is one of the earliest examples of the U-shaped plan which survived in France as the *cour d'honneur* or court of honor.

The loggia here with its mural of Cupid and Psyche was known as the Summer Loggia because it faces in a generally northern direction. On the side facing east and the Tiber, and also the main garden, was another loggia now enclosed. Its mural, The Triumph of Galatea, and other decorations were painted·by Raphael assisted by Peruzzi and Sebastiano del Piombo. This was the Garden or Winter Loggia, enclosed in the 17th century and the garden disappeared in the late 1870s with the building of high embankments for flood control and for the thoroughfare called Lungotevere Farnesina.

The state chamber, the *Sala delle Colonne,* on the *piano nobile* was decorated by Peruzzi himself. In a wholly architectural frame, which explains the reference to the trompe l'oeil columns, he depicted views of the Rome of his day. He abided by Bramante's Tempietto line for line with pilasters facing square piers.

The Renaissance has no other building which achieves such perfection in the unity of architecture and painting.

Originally, as may be guessed, the villa was open with its loggias instead of rooms, a Renaissance recreation of a Roman villa, more of a pleasure spot than a residence. Over the generations the openness disappeared, the entrance court shifted from north to south (to what had been a *giardino secreto,* a secret garden). The American Academy in Rome was offered the villa at the turn of the century, but the trustees decided it was too close to the Tiber to be healthy (shades of Henry James' *Daisy Miller*) and had McKim, Mead & White design the present academy building high on the slopes of the Janiculum behind here.

A note on Letarouilly's view of the Villa on plate 10. In the distance is a building with three arches, this is the Belvedere of the Falconiere Palace by Borromini. Then comes the great mass of the Farnese Palace, now the French Embassy. The two domes in the far distance appear to be those of San Andrèa della Valle and San Carlo di Catinari, only they have been brought much closer, than they really are, for scenic effect.

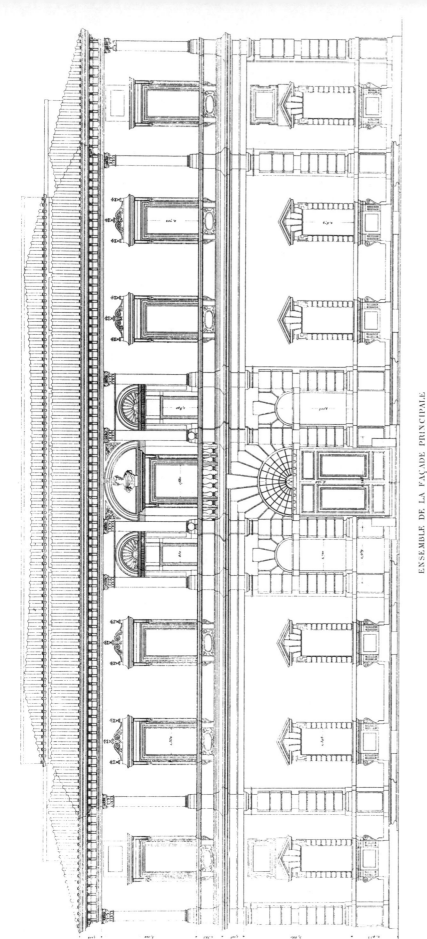

ENSEMBLE DE LA FAÇADE PRINCIPALE

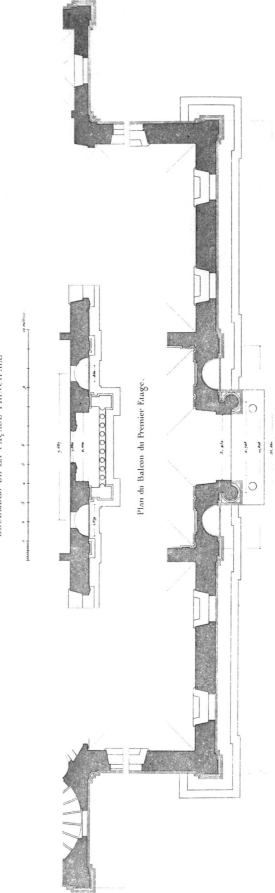

Plan du Balcon du Premier Étage.

PLATE 1. Façade of the Villa Giulia

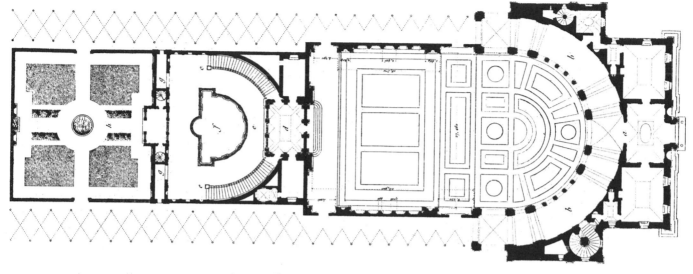

VUE DE L'ENSEMBLE DES BATIMENTS PRISE DE L'ENTREE.

PLATE 2. Plan of the Villa Giulia

89

PLATE 3. Main Court with Semicircular Portico

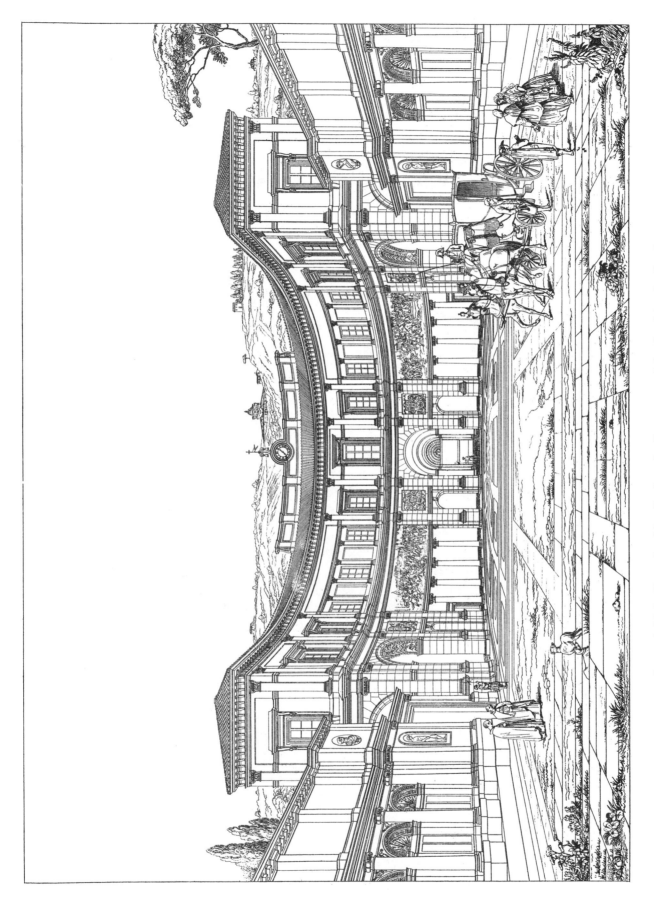

PLATE 4. Main Court Looking Back at the Entrance and the Semicircular Portico

91

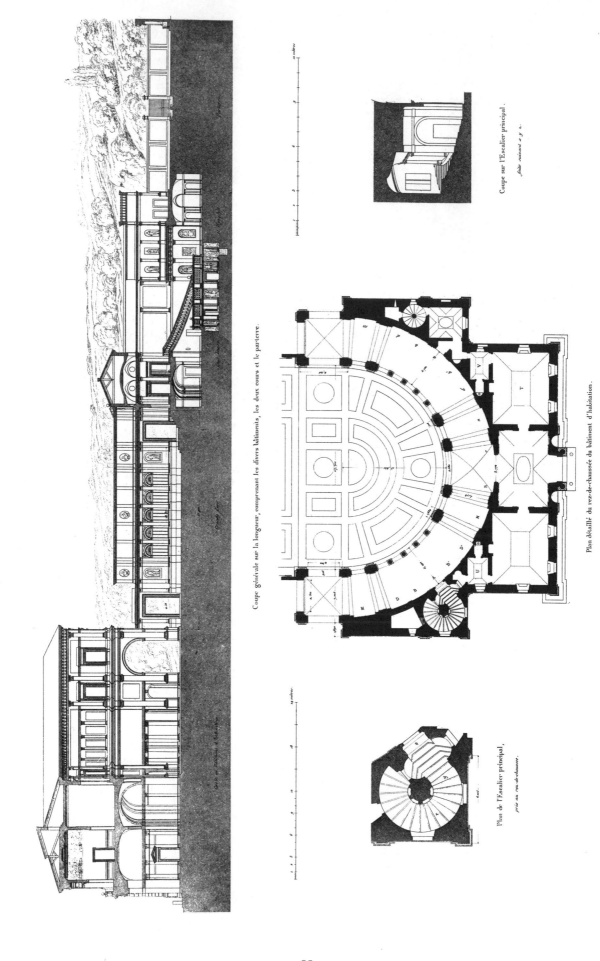

Coupe générale sur la longueur, comprenant les divers bâtiments, les deux cours et le parterre.

Coupe sur l'Escalier principal.

Plan détaillé du rez-de-chaussée du bâtiment d'habitation.

Plan de l'Escalier principal, prise au rez-de-chaussée.

PLATE 5. Longitudinal Section Down the Middle of the Villa. Plan of Main Building or Residence

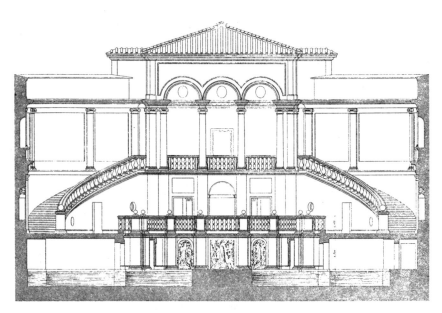

Elévation adossée à la grande cour

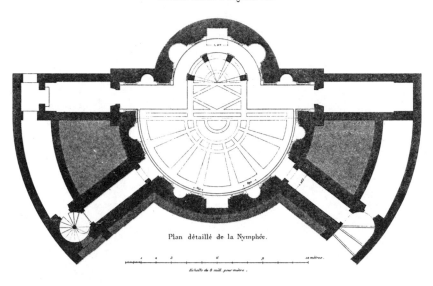

Plan détaillé de la Nymphée.

Echelle de 8 mill. pour mètre.

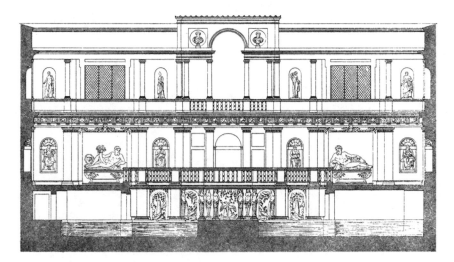

Elévation adossée au parterre.

PLATE 6. View and Plan of the Court with the Nymphaeum

93

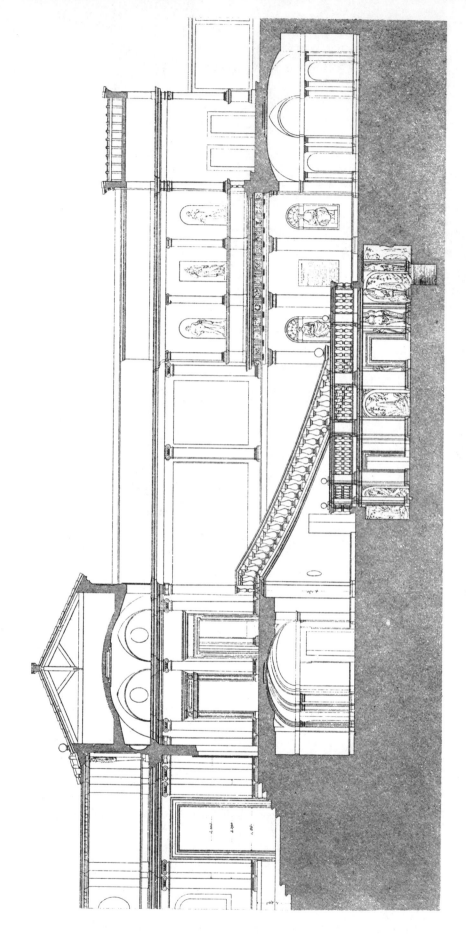

PLATE 7. Cross-Section of the Court with the Nymphaeum

Plan du Casin
de la Villa Giustiniani
et d'une partie des jardins.
I, 97.

Plan détaillé du Casin de la Villa Giustiniani.—I, 97.

J.J. Olivier et Penel sculp.

a.—Petite cour et entrée latérale.

PLATE 8. Rear Elevation of the Casino of the Villa Giustiniani/Massimo

95

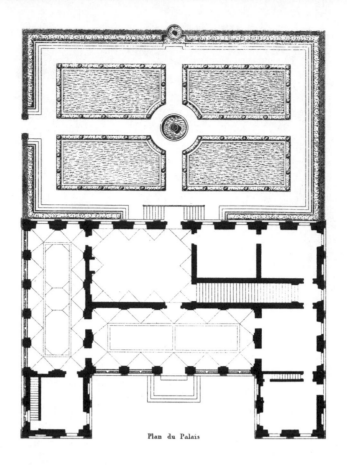

Plan du Palais

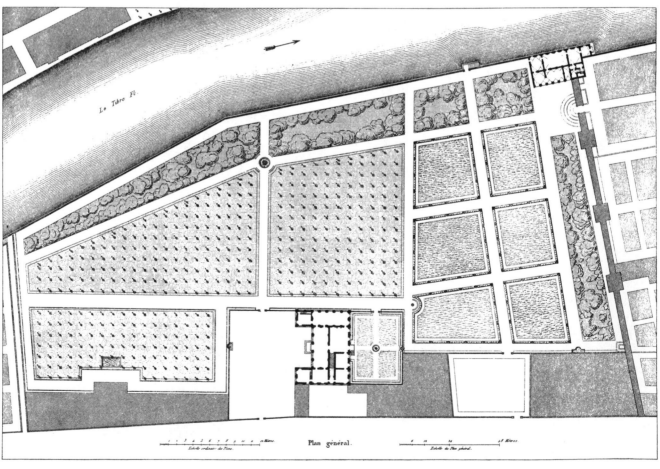

Le Tibre Fl.

Plan général.

Echelle ordinaire des Plans.

Echelle du Plan général.

Baldassarre Peruzzi.

PLATE 9. The Plan and Site of the Villa Farnesina Built by the Banker Agostino Chigi

96

PLATE 10. The Loggia of the Former Entrance Front, Now the Garden Front, with Raphael's Mural of Cupid and Psyche

Fig. 4 The School of Athens, 1510–1511, by Raphael in the *Stanza della Segnatura,* the Vatican.
Photo Courtesy Ente Provinciale di Turismo, Roma

Fig. 4-A Bramante with the calipers in "The School of Athens". Photo Courtesy Istituto Centrale
per il Catalogo e la Documentazione

As for the colonnade it is in the smallest scale compatible with accessibility, the element linked to human use. Doors and windows (plate 2) entirely fill the intervoluminations or go beyond them. It is well to recall that there is no long distance view of the Tempietto (plate 1). It is seen suddenly as soon as one enters the door of the court, at so short a distance that binocular vision estimates the measurements of the elements exactly.

The 48 metopes of the Doric entablature of the peristyle (plate 2)—with that of the Belvedere of the Vatican one of the first examples of the Doric in triglyphs in the Renaissance—has representations of twelve liturgical objects which are repeated four times. They are the chalice and paten (symbol of the bond between heaven and earth), the *padiglione* or papal umbrella (symbolic of the pope as spiritual king), the crossed keys of Saint Peter, and the incense boat (an allusion to the apostolic barque of the Church). They celebrate Saint Peter as the *Primus Pontifex* of the Church able to transmit grace through the Sacraments.

Ferdinand and Isabella of Spain had commissioned the Church of San Pietro Montorio. After his consort's death, the king had the Tempietto built.

With its crypt (plate 2) the Tempietto was originally part of a larger design. A second colonnade was to encircle the building with a tiny circular room

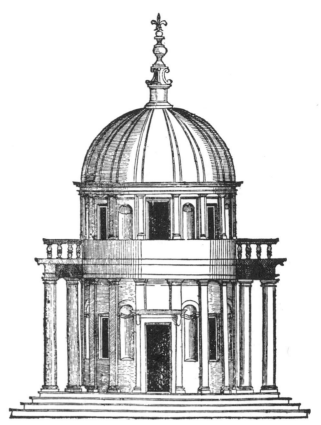

FIG. 5 Bramante's Tempietto as illustrated in Palladio, *I Quattro Libri dell'Architettura*. Courtesy American Academy in Rome

FIG. 6 Temple of Sybil at Tivoli outside of Rome. Photo Alinari/Art Resource, Inc.

FIG. 7 So-called Temple of Vesta in Rome. Wash drawing by Charles Garnier, architect of the Paris Opera House. From Hector d'Espouy, *Fragments from Greek and Roman Architecture*

101

FIG. 8 The Brooklyn Museum with its steps, 1900–1905, by McKim, Mead & White. From *Monograph of the Work of McKim, Mead & White.*

at each corner, offering an effect not too far from his plan for St. Peter's. As Serlio reminds us this martyrium was "made for the sole purpose of commemorating Saint Peter the Apostle on the spot where, it is said, he was crucified." Serlio included it in his *Della Antichita.*

The Chigi Chapel (plates 3 and 4) in Santa Maria del Popolo has a dome set over a square space by means of pendentives (a Byzantine form never used by the ancient Romans). It was designed by Raphael in 1513 for Agostino Chigi, the great banker who built the Villa Farnesina.

The mosaics of the dome (plate 5) are from drawings by Raphael. God-the-Father is at the top and around him, between the windows, are the Creation and Original Sin. The altar piece is the Birth of the Virgin, and on the frontal Jesus and the Samaritan in relief. In the niches are the prophets of the Resurrection, in the lunettes scenes from the life of David, and in the pendentives the Four Seasons.

I cite these decorations because one of the reasons for classical architecture is that it provides the best settings for "nature" which was the word that they used once to describe mankind, i.e., "Man."

The best settings are provided by classical architecture because it is immediately apprehendable. The eye can take in the plan or the elevations of a classical building at a glance. Once you could ascend the exterior grand stairway of the Brooklyn Museum (figs. 8 and 9) removed in 1936 in a moment of Modernism, and you would find yourself in a big square multistory sculpture hall. There were galleries to either side and stairs straight ahead. You knew just where you were at all times. Now with "modern circulation" you depend on illuminated arrows and signs. Looking at the facade of the museum the whole scheme with the tympanum, the triangular surface bound by the sloping and horizontal cornices of a pediment, and the statues at the attic, the upper story of the building above the main cornice, is perfectly explicit.

Classical statues and mural decorations must have an architectural setting. They and classical architecture answer to each other. The supreme ornament in classical architecture is the human figure. The next step down in the hierarchy of ornament is devoted to part-humans who serve as architectural supports, figures or half-figures (atlantes and caryatides) used instead of columns to support an entablature. Next would be heads and masks used on keystones and on shields.

FIG. 9 The Brooklyn Museum today without the steps which were removed in 1936. Photo Dick Schuler

102

After man come the lions. Has anyone counted the lion population of the New York Public Library? (fig. 10) Perhaps the lion is the most represented of beings. Think of the number of chairs and tables standing on lion paws. Sir Edwin Landseer's lions for the Nelson Column in London's Trafalgar Square may have set the vogue for lions couchant to either side of entrance ways. Lions couchant were not a Renaissance motif whereas lion masks were. Then there are the fabulous beasts. The griffon having the body of a lion and the head and wings of an eagle, the sphinx with the hindquarters of a lion and head and breast of a woman.

Now we come to Flora's realm. The first element here is the acanthus leaf. It is artificial foliage. The real acanthus leaf, and you will meet it first probably walking in the Roman Forum where it abounds, is a great disappointment. It does not look a bit the way it should, if nature follows art. The acanthus leaf is the immortal morphological symbol of the West, as the Lotus is of the East. It is the earmark of classical styles. In the Middle Ages it was formalized into a crocket or spread flat like an open hand. In the Renaissance the leaf was nuptial and elegant, in the High Renaissance it achieved the Golden Mean as at St. Peter's whose Corinthian Order is based on the Temple of Mars the Avenger (fig. 11). In the Baroque our leaf flourishes in stucco, a noble material, is fecund in column capitals, and runs riot in many wonderful ways. The apotheosis of this luminous and common leaf is to be found in the capitals of the Temple of Mars the Avenger in the Forum of Augustus. Here one can see the Virgilian majesty of Rome.

Last in the hierarchy of ornament come the geometric forms, such as the Greek fret, the guilloche.

When the moldings and ornaments of the Chigi Chapel were being made in the early 16th century the stonecutters and architects were able to consult the remains of ancient Rome. Many more were extant, and the modern city had not been built over so many of them.

What homely elements decorate this elaborate and costly room. In the entablature in plate 5, the left reading down, we have an acanthus band and egg-and-dart, and the same pair in the architrave with bead-and-reel. The Corinthian capital is made from acanthus leaves, cabbage and volutes.

Geometry comes to play in the Greek Key and the double guilloche (plate 5) in the middle of the page.

FIG. 10 One of the two lions in front of the New York Public Library. Edward Clark Potter, sculptor. Photo Dick Schuler

FIG. 11 The Corinthian capital of the Temple of Mars the Avenger in Rome. Wash drawing by Hector d'Espouy. From Hector d'Espouy, *Fragments from Greek and Roman Architecture*

103

PLATE 1. The Tempietto (1502) by Bramante

104

Elévation.

Coupe.

Plan du·rez-de-chaussée.

Echelle des Plans.

Détail de l'ordre extérieur.

Plan de la Chapelle souterraine.

Détail d'une partie de la Coupe de la Chapelle souterraine.

Echelle des détails ci-dessus.

PLATE 2. Details of the Tempietto, Showing Elevation, Cross-Section, Portion of Outside Order, Plans of Ground Floor and Subterranean Chapel, and Section of Subterranean Chapel

Pl. 238.

Voir les planches 97 et 98.

PLATE 3. The Chigi Chapel (1513) by Raphael in Santa Maria del Popolo

PLATE 4. Cross-Section of the Elevation of the Chigi Chapel and the Plan

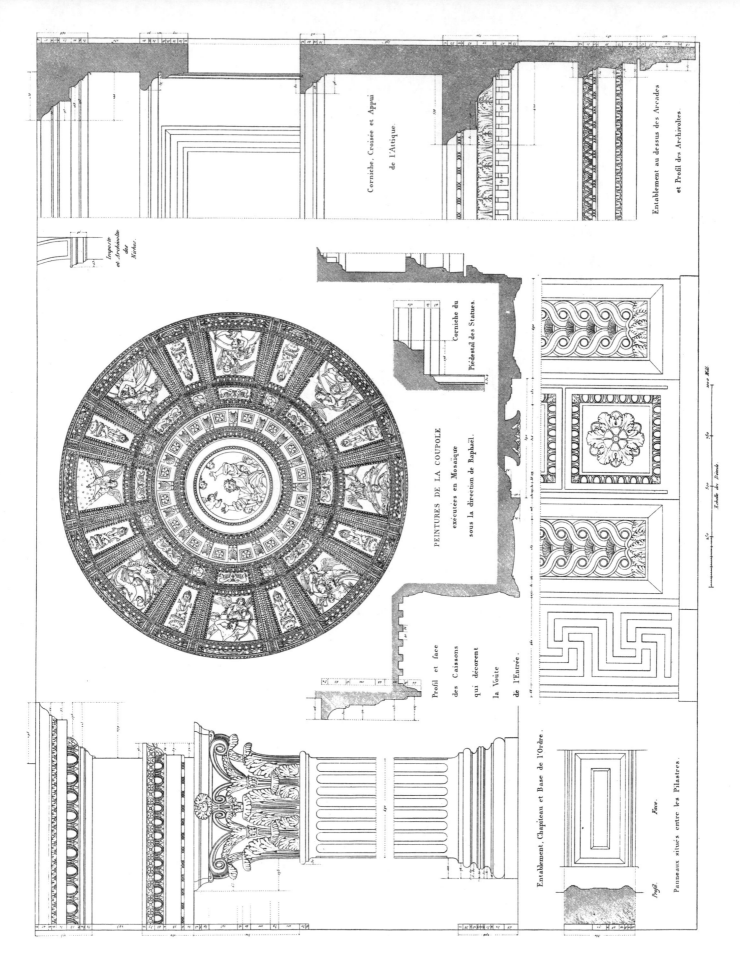

Corniche, Croisée et Appui
de l'Attique.

Entablement au dessus des Arcades
et Profil des Archivoltes.

Imposte
et Archivolte
des
Niches.

Corniche du
Piédestal des Statues.

PEINTURES DE LA COUPOLE
exécutées en Mosaïque
sous la direction de Raphaël.

Profil et face
des Caissons
qui décorent
la Voûte
de l'Entrée.

Entablement, Chapiteau et Base de l'Ordre.

Face.

Profil.

Panneaux situés entre les Pilastres.

Echelle des Détails.

PLATE 5. Details of the Chigi Chapel

X · SAINT PETER'S SQUARE

If the great square of secular Rome is on the Capitoline, the square of ecclesiastical Rome is that of St. Peter's (plate 1). It has an ellipse, the west of which opens on a truncated triangle leading to the Basilica.

The spectator who enters an ellipse as here is led to identify his sense of gesture with the wider curves spread left and right more generously than in a circle. If he enters on the cross axis the movement suggested is constrictive. For this reason the shorter axis of an ellipse should be considered the principal one.

On the very day of his election, April 7, 1655, Pope Alexander VII (Chigi) sent for Bernini and bade him draw a scheme for the colonnades. The Obelisk was already in place, having been raised on its site in 1586. The architect Carlo Maderno had made it axial with the Basilica by tilting his facade several degrees out of perpendicularity to the nave.

Bernini proposed two curved regiments of columns, the most impressive assembly of columns in the world for the ellipse. (plate 2). 280 Of them altogether, fifty feet high, they form colonnades 61 feet wide and 64 feet high (Chapter XII, plate 2).

Above is a "cloud of witnesses," 140 statues of saints about 10 feet high, occupying the skyline (plate 2). Doric simplicity (plate 3) was successfully wedded to Baroque declamation.

Many Americans, certainly New Yorkers, will recall the Pennsylvania Station (fig. 1) in New York by the well-known firm of McKim, Mead & White with its parade of granite columns along Seventh Avenue.

Bernini's piazza is joined to the Basilica facade, of Carlo Maderno, the facade to Maderno's nave, the nave to Michelangelo's and Bramante's crossing (the Pantheon married to the Temple of Concord), all on a single axis dramatically consistent. Just as crown was added to crown on the tiara of the pope, the Pontifex Maximus.

In the ellipse the fountains (plate 2) to the north and south of the obelisk, maintain their giant watershapes with the water drawn from the depths of Lake Bracciano 40 miles to the north.

The colonnades are cut off at the eastern side, opening to the Via della Conciliazione In Bernini's scheme a pavilion (fig. 2) was to stand there, but the final link was never forged.

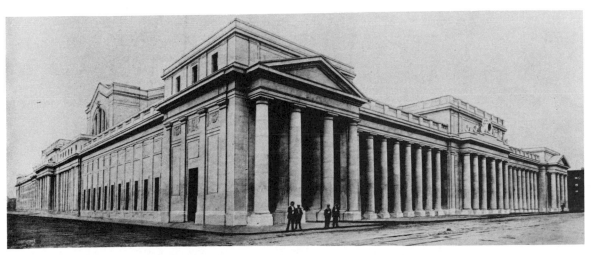

FIG. 1 View of the Seventh Avenue front of the Pennsylvania Station, 1909, in New York. McKim, Mead & White, arch. Photo George B. Hall & Son, courtesy Museum of the City of New York

109

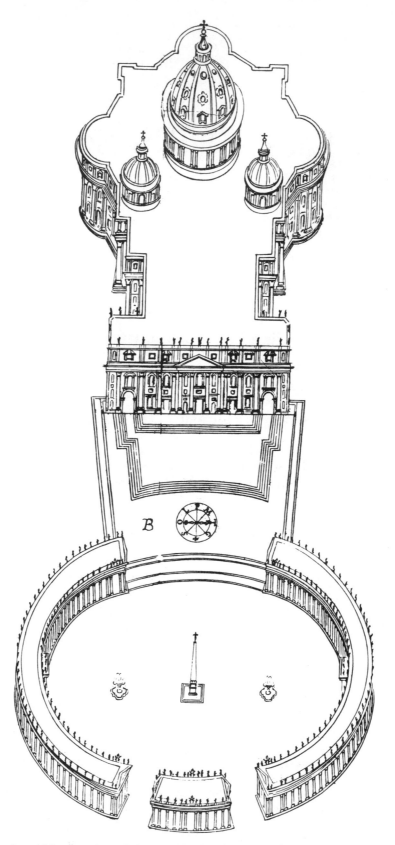

FIG. 2 Bird's eye view of St. Peter's and the square showing Bernini's pavilion at the east side which was never built. View by Giovanni Bonacina, 1659. Photo Cabinet des Estampes, Bibliothèque Nationale, Paris

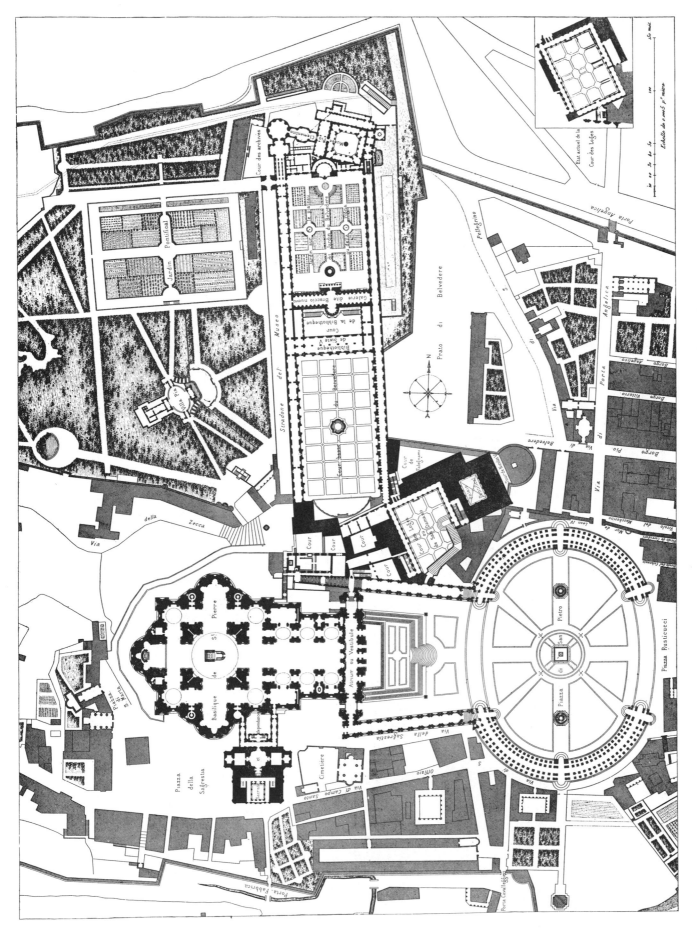

PLATE 1. Plan of the Square, the Basilica and the Vatican Palace

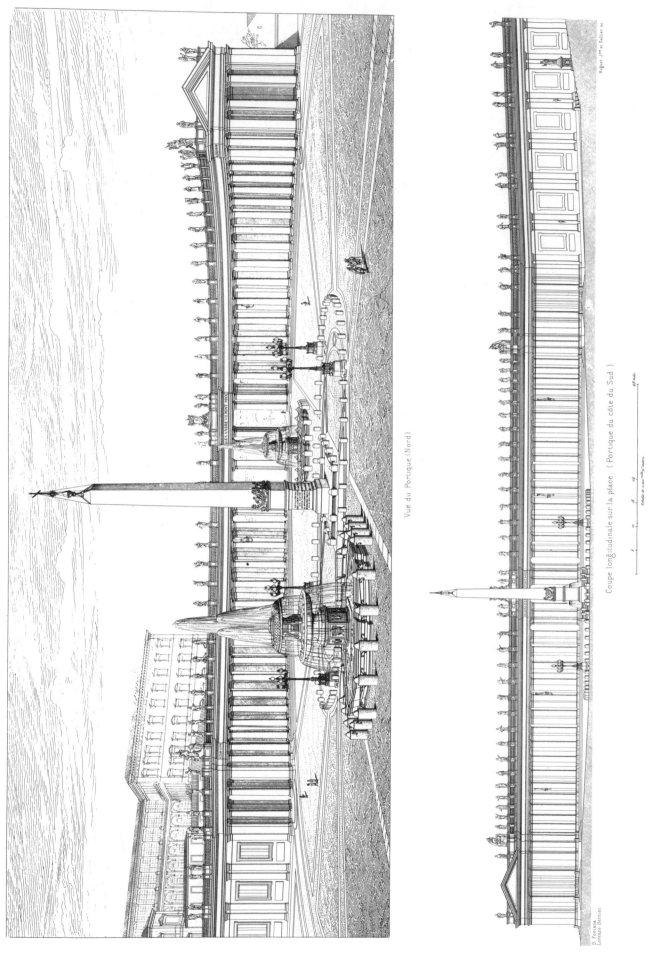

Vue du Portique (Nord)

D. Fontana,
Lorenzo Bernini

Coupe longitudinale sur la place. (Portique du côté du Sud)

Bigot J.me et Sellier sc

PLATE 2. View of the fountains, obelisk and north curve of the Ellipse. View of the South Curve of the Ellipse and the South Side of the Truncated Triangle

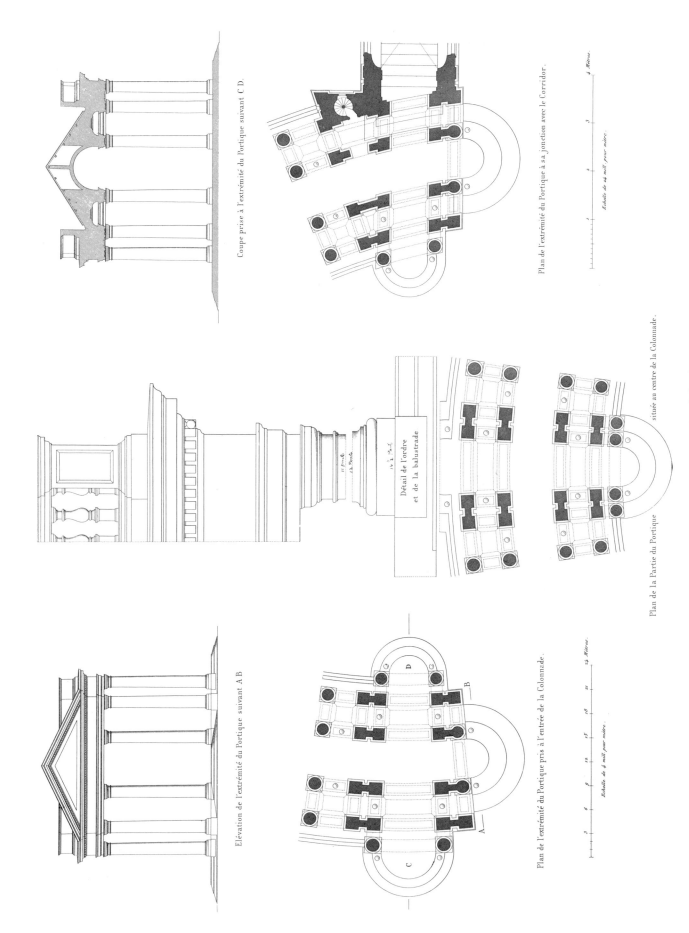

Coupe prise à l'extrémité du Portique suivant C D.

Plan de l'extrémité du Portique à sa jonction avec le Corridor.

Echelle de 24 millt pour mètre.

Détail de l'ordre et de la balustrade

Plan de la Partie du Portique située au centre de la Colonnade.

Elévation de l'extrémité du Portique suivant A B

Plan de l'extrémité du Portique pris à l'entrée de la Colonnade.

Echelle de 9 millt pour mètre.

PLATE 3. Details of the Colonnade of the Square

113

XI · SAINT PETER'S

This dome (plate 1) is one of the four small ones proposed. Two were built. The original Greek cross plan of Bramante had five domes. There were four small domes, one at each corner, if we imagine it set on a square, of the principal dome (plate 2). This same scheme was continued by Michelangelo (plate 3).

The two domes that were built are east of the great dome (Chapter X, fig. 2). They constitute the north-east and the south-east angles of Michelangelo's plan. As you will see from the section they are really not expressed as interiors visible from inside the basilica. They serve merely to cover the rather small hole which admits light to the chapel below. They were built by Giacomo della Porta working for Clement VIII (Aldobrandini) pope from 1592 to 1605. On Clement's death the Michelangelo scheme was finally forsaken, and it was decided to prolong the nave, and have a Latin cross plan (plate 4). With the lengthening of the nave these domes are barely visible from the piazza. The two domes to the west of the great dome were never built (see Chapter X, fig. 2). We present them as rather *professional* domes that can be realized at almost any scale. They were long attributed to Vignola who was the first 'professional' architect. That is he was not a painter or sculptor as well. We can understand why this dome was given to Vignola. It has his look of 'golden mean', of balance, of "juste milieu" or happy medium which are the qualities that make his work such an excellent basis for study and imitation (plates 1 and 5).

We leave the vestibule (fig. 1) and enter the nave (fig. 2), if you will, by the door in the background just behind the statue of St. Peter to the right of the pier (plate 6).

One's first impression is one of slight dismay. We are not used to brightly lighted churches. We are used to the dim light of the Gothic Revival, to devotional gloom and spookiness. Here the sublime mysteries of Christianity are performed in the broad daylight with tourists trailing about with their guidebooks oblivious to everything but history.

The mysteries of primitive cults are secret, veiled, mysterious. Here we have the triumph of light—explicit, lucid, humane (thanks to Western theology and art)—over primitive darkness shrouded, esoteric, magical.

"In Gothic churches the inclination is to kneel with one's hands joined in humble prayer and in deep regret. In Saint Peter's, on the other hand, the instinctive gesture would be to throw open one's arms in joy, raise one's head in happiness and radiance. . . ." (From the French by Eugénie de la Ferronays as cited by Augustus J.C. Hare in *Walks in Rome*.) Something of this feeling can be enjoyed at Grand Central's "Grand Concourse" in New York.

Critics always "go on" about the dimensions of St. Peter's, and how they are hard to comprehend, the height of the nave is that of a fifteen-story building, the vestibule is five hundred feet long, and so on. In truth St. Peter's is only itself when the Pope is at the high altar, and the building thronged with worshippers. Then its immensity is immediately apparent.

The pier on the left is one of four stupendous piers that hold up the dome. They were established by Bramante in 1506, as one of the first elements of the new St. Peter's. They were strengthened by Michelangelo in 1546, and the niches top and bottom scooped out by Bernini in 1628.

Our pier (plate 6) is that of St. Longinus whose statue is by Bernini. In his right hand the soldier saint holds the lance that pierced Christ's side. The relic was presented by the Sultan of Turkey. The niches are occupied by statues of four sacred figures. Their relics are kept in rooms over them, and the relics are exposed from the balconies on Feast Days.

The twisted columns above once surrounded the grave of St. Peter in the old basilica. They were placed there ". . . vine-clad columns brought from Greece . . ." by the Emperor Constantine. They are of translucent marble, and monolithic, including the capitals and bases, carved around the year 200. The vine leaves are Dionysiac. They transpose easily enough into the Lord's vineyard.

Now let us examine the Order of the nave . . . The pilasters are eighty-three feet high, and the entablature twenty-feet high. This titanic Order was created by Michelangelo.

The next point I would like to make is not illustrated in Letarouilly. It is the effect of the nave as seen from the entrance (fig. 2). You look down over an expanse of inlaid marbles to the baldachino, and through it to the shrine of the Chair of Saint Peter. The effect is of infinity. The Holy of Holies emphasized by the dome. No windows are to be seen except in the drum of the dome.

The point I want to make has to do with "doublure," the difference between the exterior and the interior, it being French for lining as in the lining of a garment. The thickness of the walls is about twelve feet. This gives a margin for play or "doublure,"—and not one window fits an exterior opening. Interior and exterior do not fit; they do not have to fit. There are semicircular lunettes over some of the altars, and the window giving them light is rectangular. The interior windows of the three apses, on the *piano nobile* usually have heavy dark red curtains hung behind the glass of the interior windows, otherwise you would see the ceiling of the passage in the thickness of the wall.

The nave is lighted by dormers. Letarouilly's engravers have omitted them. The aisles are lighted by domes with cupolas. These are barely perceptible through the arches on the right of our print. Over the segmental arches which separate the bays you will see a window or a void (fig. 3). These are, in fact, filled with wooden partitions painted to look like windows. The window over the head of Saint Peter on the end wall should have glazing bars. It looks into the vast Hall of Benedictions which is over the portico.

The reclining women in the spandrels of the nave arches are accompanied by attributes, some of which

FIG. 1 The Portico of Saint Peter's. Engraving by Giuseppe Vasi, after Francesco Panini, 1763.
With permission of The Metropolitan Museum of Art, Rogers Fund, 1966

FIG. 2 The nave of Saint Peter's. Engraving by Giovanni Battista Piranesi, 1748.
With permission of The Metropolitan Museum of Art, Harris Brisbane Dick Fund, 1937

are gilded. The one holding a cross with a dog at her feet represents Religious Faith, while her neighbor with a rose in her right hand and a unicorn besides her is Chastity. Divine Justice holds a flaming sword with a globe at her feet. Another with a crown of flowers and a lamb in her bosom is Gentleness. All are of stucco.

The ceiling is in gilt stucco. The Order and the entablature are of white marble; the frieze is gilt. The six-foot letters are actually in paper cut out and painted a purple blue. The columns of the aisles are of red and white marble.

"The interior burst upon our astonished gaze, resplendent in light, magnificence and beauty, beyond all that imagination can conceive . . . As I walked slowly up its long nave, empanelled with the rarest and richest marbles and adorned with the art of sculpture and of taste . . . I felt it was indeed unparalleled in beauty, in magnitude, and magnificence and one of the noblest and most wonderful works of man." (The passage is from *Rome In the Nineteenth Century* by Charlotte A. Eaton as cited by Augustus J.C. Hare in his *Walks in Rome*.)

This dome (plate 7) is the greatest creation of the Renaissance. A dome over the prince of Apostles was proposed in mid-Fifteenth century. Bramante had made a dome which we have examined at San Pietro in Montorio in 1502, but for the Basilica of St. Peter he designed a Pantheon saucer dome on a ring of columns (plate 8). Then Sangallo came along with a wedding cake of columns and not much dome, and an enormous lantern (plate 9). Michelangelo designed an absolutely distinct drum (plate 10) which presented the problem in statics which the older man shied away from. He took the double-shell construction from Brunelleschi's dome (see the dome of the Cathedral in Florence in Figure 3 of Chapter IX, "Domes"), plus the ribs, the windows in the dome, and the octagonal lantern. The inside shell has always been hemispherical. The outside was redesigned after his death in 1564. Sixtus V (Peretti) who ruled from 1585 to 1590 had Giacomo della Porta make a full-size drawing of the new profile on paper. It was spread out on the floor of St. Paul's-outside-the-Walls, the largest space available, studied by the Pope from a balcony, and approved. The drum is buttressed with spur walls

FIG. 3 View of the south aisle looking west in Saint Peter's. Watercolor by Louis Haghe, 1864, in the Bethnal Green Museum, London. It shows the segmental arches and the window openings a void filled with wood partitions painted to resemble windows. Photo Victoria and Albert Museum, London

perpendicular to it with columns at either corner backed by pilasters. In our plate (plate 7) you can spot the spur wall by the little round-headed access opening in it. It is actually ten feet high, and they show an accent of daylight and give certain lightening at a point where statically weight is not needed. The tops of the piers were to have been linked to the drum by scrolls, and the thrust of the buttresses against the drum strengthened by additional weight at a crucial point in the form of statues of prophets. I have sketched these last elements into our plate. If the buttress in the plate doesn't seem to project very much it is because the section was taken through the middle of the dome, and the buttress is already half a bay around the corner.

Below what we see on our plate are the four awe-inspiring arches which carry everything before us (fig. 4). On the pendentives between the arches are round *tondi* pictures of the four Evangelists. Our plate begins with the entablature over the arches. In the frieze there is an inscription in mosaic, dark blue letters on a gold ground. "Tu es Petrus et super hanc petram aedificabo ecclesiam meam et tibi dabo claves regni caelorum." (You are Peter, and on this rock I will build my Church and give you the Keys to Heaven.)

Above a pedestal there are sixteen windows between coupled pilasters (plate 7). They carry the terminal cornice with its attic to the springing of the dome. The dome is divided into sixteen panels decorated in mosaic. They are divided six times horizontally.

In the lunettes sanctified Popes and Fathers of the Church. Then come great seated figures: The Redeemer, Our Lady, St. Joseph, John the Baptist and the twelve Apostles. Above them angels with symbols, then *tondi* with the heads of seraphim, the highest of nine orders of angels, another series of angels, and a last row with seraphim. In the lantern, and out of the picture, is the Eternal Father blessing the world.

The color-scheme of the whole ensemble is gold and blue. They dominate. The figures modify this with flesh tints and costumes in green, lavender, white etc., and the window enframements, the pilaster shafts and parts of the entablatures are the color of white marble.

"But when, having traversed the length of the nave without uttering a word, he passed from under the gilded roofs, and the spacious dome, lofty as a firmament, expanded itself above him in the sky, covered with tracery of the celestial glories, and brilllant with mosaic and stars of gold . . ." (The passage is from *John Inglesant* by John Henry Shorthouse as cited by Augustus J. C. Hare in his *Walks in Rome.*)

FIG. 4 Looking north from the south transept to the crossing. Watercolor by Louis Haghe in the Bethnal Green Museum, London. Photo Victoria and Albert Museum, London

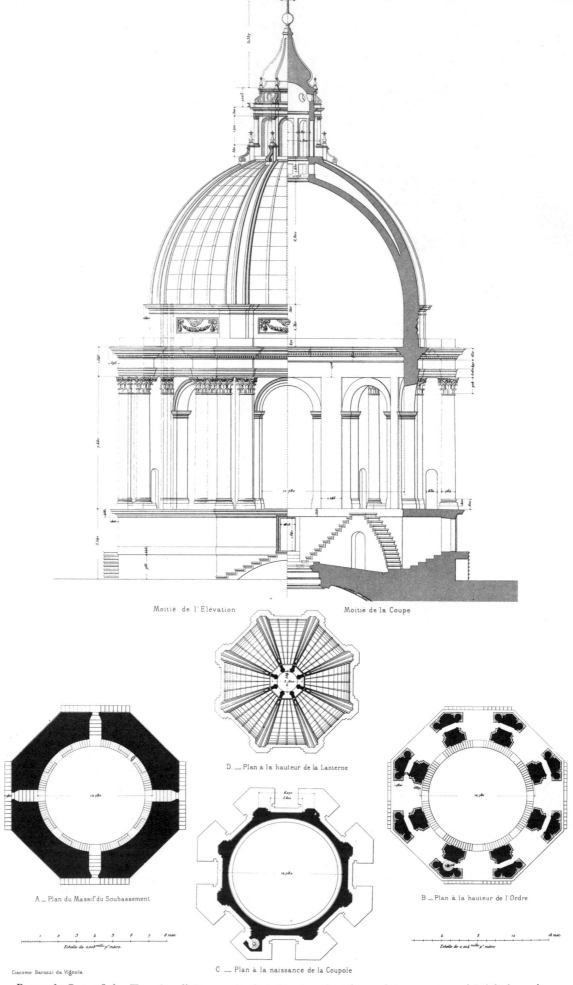

Moitié de l'Élévation

Moitié de la Coupe

D. — Plan a la hauteur de la Lanterne

A — Plan du Massif du Soubassement

C. — Plan à la naissance de la Coupole

B — Plan à la hauteur de l'Ordre

Giacomo Barozzi da Vignola

PLATE 1. One of the Two Small Domes Built Following the Plans of Bramante and Michelangelo.

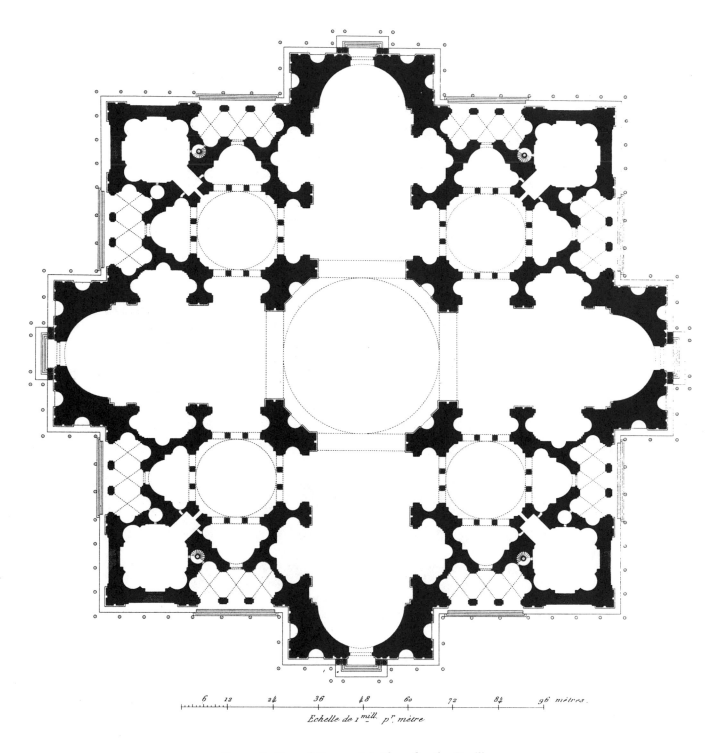

6   12   24   36   48   60   72   84   96 mètres.

Echelle de 1 mill. pr. mètre

PLATE 2. One of Bramante's Plans for the Basilica

121

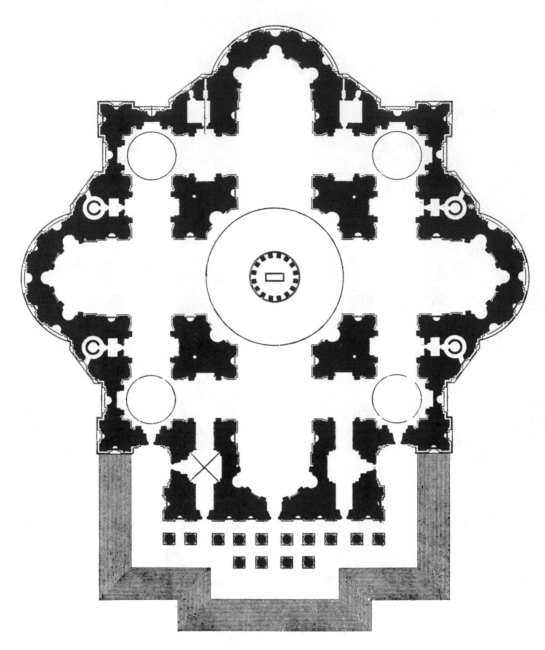

PLATE 3. Michelangelo's Plan for the Basilica

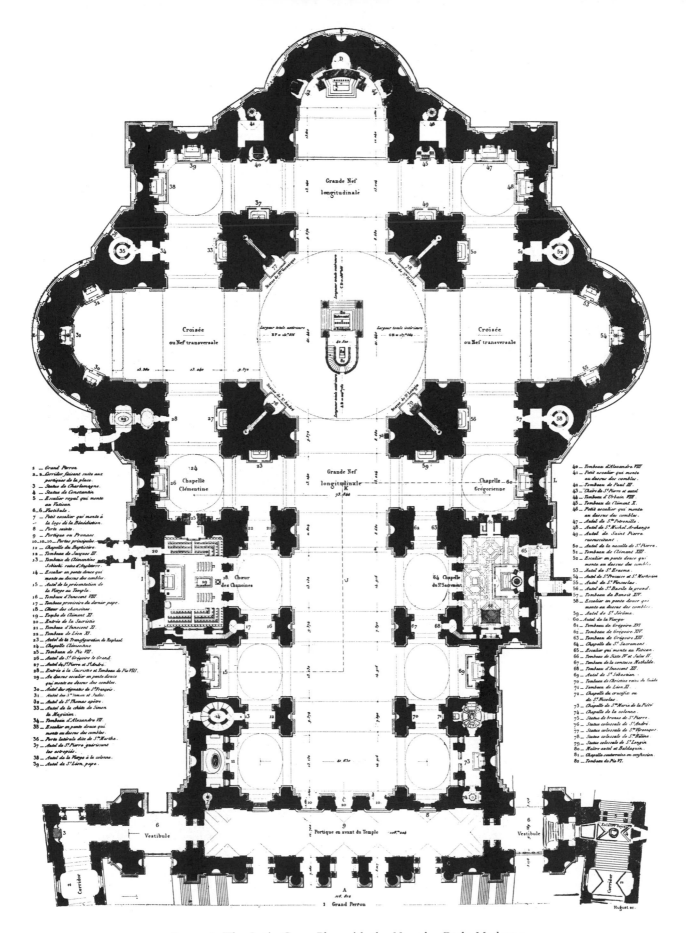

PLATE 4. The Latin Cross Plan with the Nave by Carlo Maderno

123

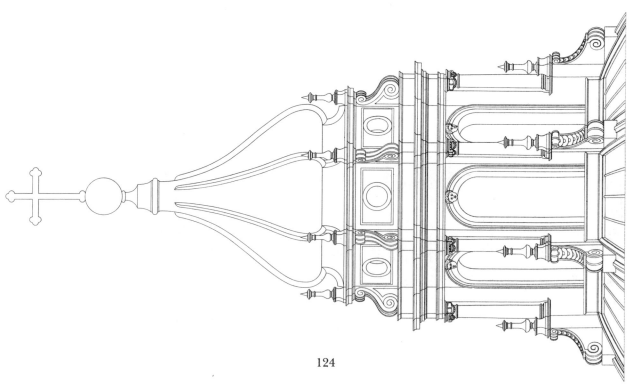

BASILIQUE DE SAINT-PIERRE.

PL. 58.

Plan du couronnement.

6 Mèt.

Echelle de 0.016 p. 1 Mèt.

3 Mèt.

Echelle de 0.014 p. 1 Mèt.

Plan au niveau de la base
de l'ordre de la lanterne.

Coupe de la lanterne.

Giacomo Barozzi da Vignola.

Élévation de la lanterne.

Maurice sc.

PLATE 5. Lantern of the Small Domes

PLATE 6. One of the Four Great Piers, the Northeast One, Beneath the Dome. The Statue of Saint Longinus by Bernini Is in the Niche

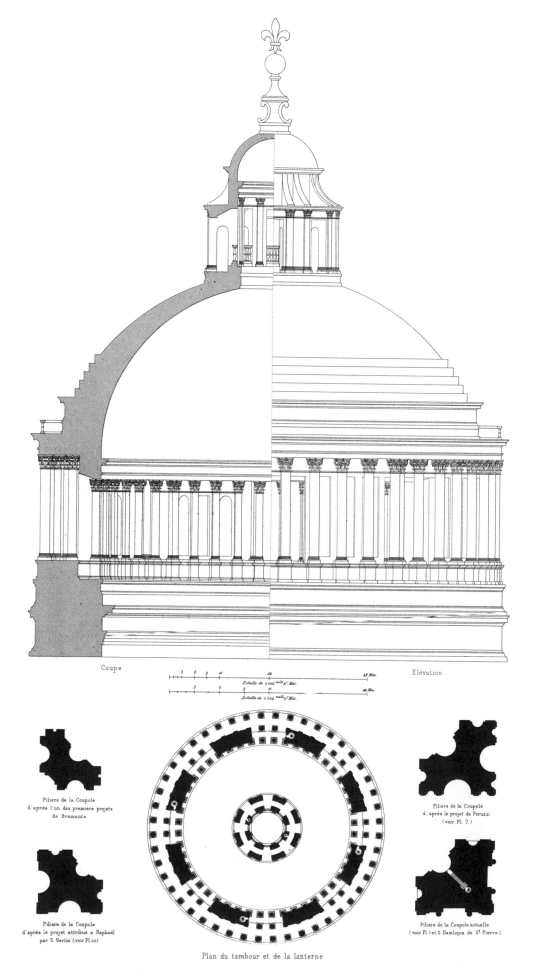

Coupe

Echelle de 0,002 milli p.ᵉ Mᵉᵗ.

Echelle de 0,004 milli p.ᵉ Mᵉᵗ.

Elévation

Piliers de la Coupole
d'après l'un des premiers projets
de Bramante.

Piliers de la Coupole
d'après le projet de Peruzzi
(voir. Pl. 7.)

Piliers de la Coupole
d'après le projet attribué a Raphaël
par S. Serlio (voir Pl.10.)

Piliers de la Coupole actuelle
(voir Pl. 1 et 2. Basilique de Sᵗ Pierre.)

Plan du tambour et de la lanterne

PLATE 8. The Dome and Drum of Bramante according to Serlio

Echelle de 2 mill. pour mètre.

Projet définitif d'Antonio da Sangallo.

Plan
de
la façade
ci-dessus

Chappuis sc.

PLATE 9. The Dome by Antonio da Sangallo

Imp Lemoureux. Paris

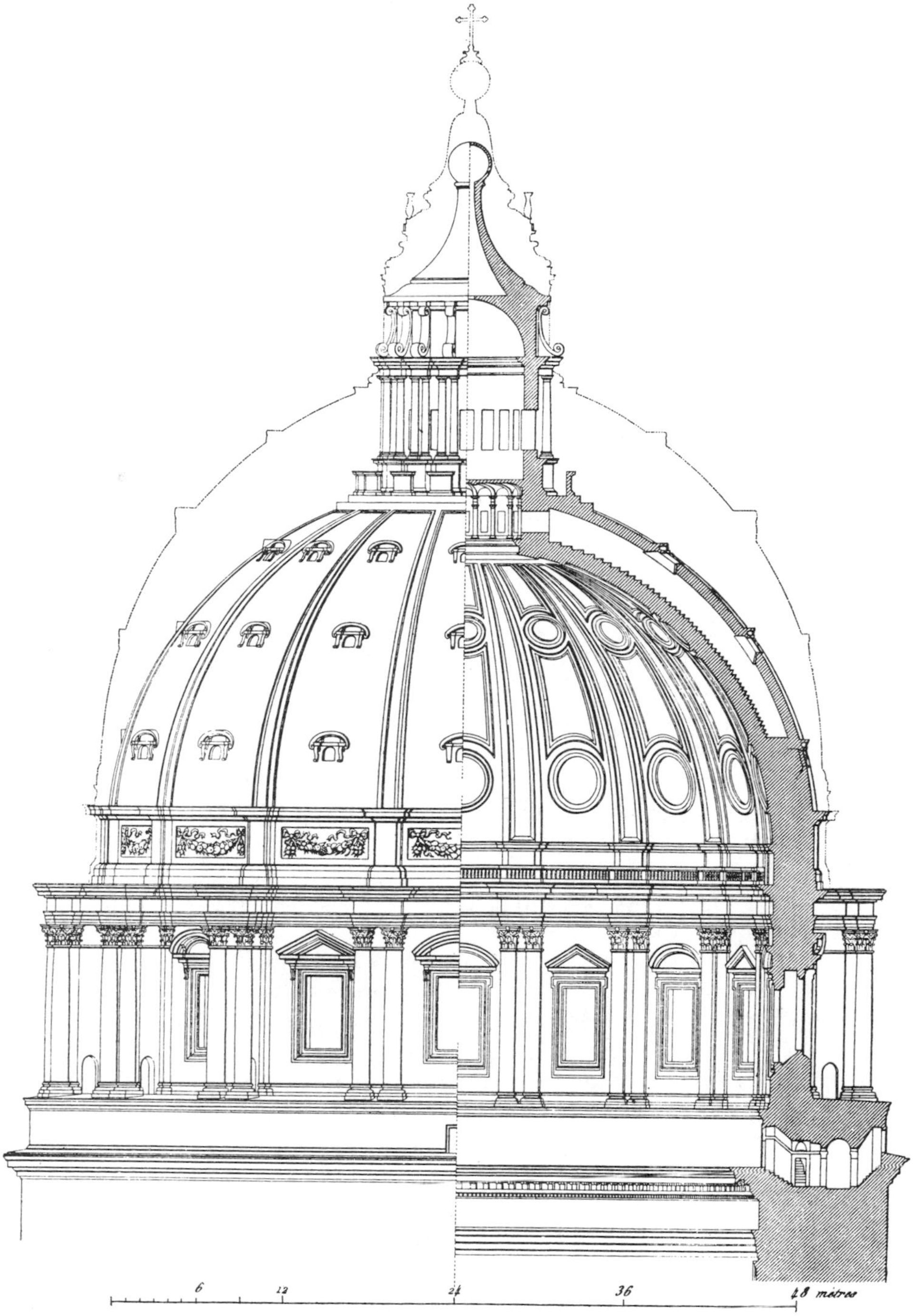

Plate 10. The Dome by Michelangelo

XII · THE VATICAN

The Vatican is the largest palace in the world. It has eight grand staircases and twenty courts, and is said to contain eleven thousand rooms.

If you are having an audience with the Pope, you may walk across the Piazza San Pietro leaving the obelisk to your left, and you go to the "Portone di Bronzo" (plate 1) It is at the far end of the great curving colonnade that frames the north side of the Piazza. If you will turn to plate 2 you will see the inside of the colonnade; walk to the end of it, and you will be at the 'Bronze Door'. From here the 'Corridor of Bernini' runs straight for about a hundred yards to the point where the Pontifical Palace (plates 3 and 4) begins. The picture you see would present itself after you have shown your credentials to the Swiss guard, and crossed the threshold of the palace.

This is the Royal Stairway, *Scala Regia*. It is the work of Gian Lorenzo Bernini, built 1663–6. Over the inner archway where the steps begin after the first landing is the coat of arms of Alexander VII (Chigi). The winged figures are 'Fames'. They are blowing on trumpets. With their free hands they are supporting the coat of arms.

The sculpture group by Karl Bitter (fig. 1), found on the old New York Custom House on Bowling Green, is based on this.

If the visitor enters the portico of the basilica and faces left, he will see the equestrian statue of Charlemagne (plate 5), and if he faces to the right he will see the equestrian statue of Constantine (plate 3) by Bernini. The matching statues at either end of a distance of about 400 feet establish a dramatic cross-axis to the axis of the basilica.

The poet Byron, standing one morning in the portico, overheard an Englishman, who had mistaken the statues for those of Peter and Paul, re-

mark to a friend, "I never knew that Paul rode again after his dreadful accident."

Charlemagne was crowned Holy Roman Emperor by Leo III in 800. The church was indebted to him for his ecclesiastical reforms throughout his extensive empire.

Constantine recognized Christianity as the official religion of the Roman Empire. His policy was to unite church and state. He ordered that Sunday became a public holiday.

This aisled and vaulted stairway (plate 3) on either side is the finest there is. It surpasses in dignity and in design the great baroque stairways of Germany. As you ascend this greatest of stairways on some great occasion, like the reception for the Queen of England or the President of a major state, there will be Swiss guards at intervals in red, yellow and blue stripes (Medici colors) with breast plates, ruffs, plumed helmets and halberds. If His Holiness comes by they pound the ferrules of their halberds on the marble floor very loudly—bang, bang, bang,—and everyone sinks to one knee as His Holiness passes by. The Swiss guards are marvelous scale figures throughout the Vatican City, and the other uniforms, the footmen in raspberry cut velvet with knee-breeches, style 'ancien regime,' the gendarmes in Napoleonic uniforms, the Palatine guards looking Spanish-American War period, the private secretaries looking like French Academicians except that the uniform is in navy blue rather than green, chamberlains looking like British Diplomats in scarlet jackets laced with gold and black trousers, not to mention Prince Chigi (I am writing of the 1940s) in a black Spanish Philip IV style costume with a breastplate by Cellini—all play their architectural role.

The statue of the Emperor Constantine is on the

FIG. 1 The sculpture group Karl Bitter on the attic of the United States Custom House on Bowling Green, New York City. Photo Dick Schuler

right hand side of plate 3. Bernini took the moment when the emperor saw in the sky, it was during the crucial Battle of the Milvian Bridge, a flaming cross with the words, "In this sign thou shalt conquer." The horse is rearing back as if it had seen a flash of lightning. Its mouth gapes open. The veins in its belly stand out boldly, as it rears on its hind legs. The emperor sits on the horse in the ancient manner without stirrups. He is enveloped in voluminous drapery much agitated. Both his hands are raised in astonishment at the miracle in the sky. His head is thrown backwards a little, and his mouth is slightly open as he seems to say, "Behold." Horse and rider are silhouetted against a vast curtain. It has theatrical or architectural dimensions. It is gathered at the top in heavy folds that rest on top of a canopy with a fringed valance in painted plaster. It streams down behind the horse and rider, and is being violently tossed about by a strong wind from the west. It has a deep fringe at the bottom

and it purports to be cloth of some enormously heavy kind, as the folds are monumental. Actually, the curtain is made out of plaster and covered with a tegument of wafer-thin pieces of *rosso antico* marble. It is highly polished, and a deep red color, the emperor and horse are in neutral marble.

The whole composition is set into an arch. The arch has splayed sides with the imposts (entablatures) sloped down at the rear to give an effect of depth, feigned perspective being a favorite Baroque resource. The soffit of the arch is lined with coffers with rosettes.

The two groins that let the arches into the vault, the arch over 'Constantine' and the one opposite, contain medallions in bas-relief: one shows his baptism, the other Constantine laying the foundation stone of St. Peter's. The medallions are supported by youths kneeling on the extrados, the outer curve of an arch, with a festoon of leaves.

You will observe as you look up the staircase that

131

the sides converge, you may also examine the plan where it is more obvious. From the section you can see that the columns of the colonnade diminish as they mount the slope. The higher they go, the shorter they get. The columns at the top are five feet shorter than the ones at the bottom, and the space between the columns narrows accordingly. We must also remember that the dentils of the cornices, and the coffers of the vaulting follow suit. Midway up the stairs you can perceive an arch with stars around its extrados. There is a skylight at this point that lights the landing below, and this landing and light mitigate the long perspective.

At the top of the stairs under the window there is a landing, we turn right on this and double back up the next flight (plate 4). This flight is narrower, and the walls are articulated with paired-pilasters. They diminish in height, but the walls do not converge. The ceiling heights, floor to the top of the vault, are 33 feet at the beginning of the stairway by the Constantine memorial, and 24 feet at the top where we enter the Royal Hall, *Sala Regia*. From this room doors open into the Sistine Chapel and into the Hall of Blessings, *Aula delle Benedizione*, whose height can be gauged from this cross-section (plate 5) which, facing south, shows the equestrian statue of Charlemagne in the portico below.

Circumstances of architectural grandeur are on all sides, sculpture, painting and very great design. We will never have opportunities such as this. Due to the lack of any Establishment and the absence of any 'school,' of any continuity, each of us is an autodidact, and if great opportunities were given us our struggle would be of the romantic order, a personal onslaught on the problem where the struggle is of more interest than the result. What a contrast to the work of "the grave old Italian," (the words are Christopher Wren's), who was at work for fifty years surrounded by the great exemplars of art, with a trained cadre, in the service of—among others—eight Popes and two kings.

Since a classical habitation is, to all intents, a box with holes punched in it (windows), it follows that the borders and edges/frames are what tell. There is not much design to the surface of the box other than stone-jointing, or brickwork, or the color of the stucco. There are the vertical borders, the corners. They may be strengthened by quoins, as at the Farnese Palace, or by a simple pier motif, as they are here. Then there are the horizontals, the cornice and the base. The cornice's role is self-evident, it is a form—it always projects at an angle

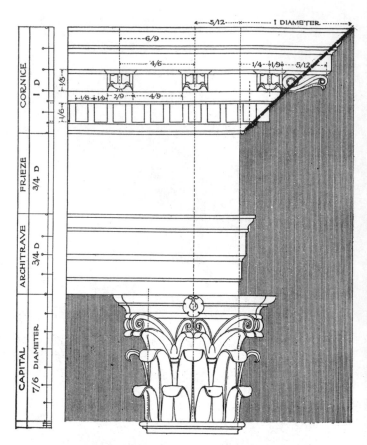

Fig. 2 Design for a Corinthian entablature showing the cornice projection at 45 degrees. From William R. Ware, *The American Vignola*

of forty-five degrees (fig. 2)—that can be infinitely varied. Matching it at the base of the facade we have a treatment which looks strong and massive enough to carry the building. In the facade before us the bottom is missing because it is jammed up against the outer wall of Bernini's oval Piazza San Pietro. Between the great horizontals of cornice and base there are the stringcourses.

The window enframements often sit on a dado that rests on the stringcourses; often on the top floor the windows are completely independent of the stringcourse, as here. There is a hierarchy in all classical things. In windows it would go from the be-columned and pedimented aedicule to the pedimented frame as here, to the frame alone, and to the simplest separation of the opening from the brick or stuccoed wall.

The second window (plate 6) in from the corner on the *piano nobile* is the window where you see photographs of the Pope greeting or blessing the people (Fig. 3). He is a small white figure with arms upraised. The window opening (plate 7) is 10 feet high, and the ceiling is about 35 feet high. We are heading towards a discussion of scale but I should like to digress on the ceiling height.

The ceilings are coffered and are made of wood painted. The depths of the coffers are the depths of the beams. The cross-pieces which form the square coffers are non-structural and decorative. Below the ceiling there is a frieze about six feet deep with a molding below it. The frieze is of painted canvas or it may be in fresco showing pictures in feigned frames supported by youths with festoons and the usual decorative properties. Below this the wall is covered with a damask with a six foot or so repeat. The reason for using damask rather than velvet or satin is that a damask pattern always picks up the light and 'reads'; a pattern is always visible. When the light strikes it from one side the background will be dark and the pattern bright, and vice versa when the light comes from the other direction. It is a positive and negative effect. The pattern always 'reads,' and this gives scale. The cloth ends at the dado, often and very wrongly called a chair-rail. (This implies that it is the height of the back of a chair. It has nothing to do with chairs.) Its height is fixed by the height of the room.

Edith Wharton and Ogden Codman in *The Decoration of Houses* wrote ". . . the interior walls are invariably treated as an Order. In well-finished rooms the Order is usually imagined as resting, not on the floor, but on pedestals, or rather on a continuous pedestal. This continuous pedestal, or *dado* as it is usually called, is represented by a plinth surmounted by mouldings." In *The American Vignola* Part II, Plate XIV (fig. 4) gives a clear idea of this important rule that the interior wall is an Order.

When the Pope looks out of the window we realize what a big window it is, and we say, "Look what big scale that building has." All the elements have the same effect. If we see someone standing beside a dado the height of his shoulder, we realize that it is a very big room. Then there are the "Scale Figures." Architects put a man or men into an elevation of a building—drawn to the same scale—to show how big the building really is. "Scale Figures" will tell you a lot about the architect. In the 1940s at the Harvard School of Design we used to scribble little things that looked like cloves because we did not know how to draw anything else, and we did not think it was important. Later we thought we should have more popular appeal, and we drew men in tweed coats sucking on pipes and Radcliffe

girls with sweaters, tweed skirts and woolen stockings; there was a lot of wool. These were the rentier-academic inhabitants of our Bauhaus housing projects. In Letarouilly the scale figures are equally revealing. They show a change of taste over a period of about thirty years. The plates done in the 1840s have people in contemporary dress: Priests in tricornes, ladies in bonnets with plumes, a hunter in a cap with his gun and dog, "Swiss" (porter of a palace, or of a church to assure order) in cocked hats with plumes, braided coats, knee breeches and swords, gentlemen in top hats, and artists in top hats. Thirty years later in the 1870s in the Vatican series everything is "period"; there are Renaissance courtiers in slashed doublets and velvet caps, peasant-women-with-child looking like Raphael madonnas, shepherds with sandals laced to the knee in reverent attitudes before a statue in the Vatican gallery, artists in the mold of Goethe with floppy hats and cloaks wrapped toga-wise.

FIG. 3 Pope John Paul II at the window of the papal apartments in the Palace of Sixtus V (Peretti) at the Vatican. Photo Anne Day

Scale figures show how big things are, but if you make a building enormous—like a factory or aeroplane hangar—it may not look big because the eye cannot find anything to measure it by, and it becomes terribly oppressive like the glass office buildings we all know and hate. How big should windows be, how wide staircases, how high the ceiling? There is functional scale; necessities are met and no more. 'Modern' architecture can supply minimals inoffensively enough, but when the bow is drawn hard back and is aimed high, the arrow falls very short of any conceivable target, as we see in the 'Grand' staircase of the Metropolitan Opera, at Lincoln Center. There are many more instances throughout the whole of that forlorn cultural supermarket.

What are the conceivable targets? Why have these extravagantly high ceilings and everything so much bigger than need be? What is the point of Roman scale? Functional scale sees man as a biological or economic unit, but it oppresses the spirit. Domestic scale is limited to a feeling of shelter. Roman scale conveys feelings of grandeur. It testifies to the formidable wills and imperious energies of soldiers, lawyers, administrators, priests and gentlemen. It is heroic and leaves the beholder with a vision of a world by noble expressions of Man's mind. A building without scale may have vast size but convey a feeling of smallness multiplied—not greatness.

Roman scale is spouse of the forms inherited from Antiquity whose rediscovery always brings new life to the vision of Imperial Rome; these forms have no connection with time, place or any exterior necessity, but by transcribing Man's will to cosmos in terms of architecture, grasp fully the humane basis, and consequent imperium of architectural art.

Classical architecture is an unconscious transcription of the body's states into forms of building, and also of the mind's states. It transcribes via style one view of the world, and the world is not about to be reinvented. Our world-view, our will to cosmos, is based on the Judeo-Christian Graeco-Roman tradition, the tradition of the West, and its associations. Classical architecture has been described as symmetrical and having lots of ornament and figure sculpture. This could be a description of Angkor Wat. Or, and now we will descend to the architecture of P.R. (the good old emperor's clothes), almost anything will be described as classical (as long as it is in vogue), and we have Yale boxes called "Palladian." I do not think there is a pat definition of classical architecture. Roman ar-

chitecture was axial, it depended heavily on sculpture as a vehicle for its moral quality, and without this its not Roman. Its themes are Sacred History and Mythology.

The circumstances of grandeur, that is, tombs, churches, palaces, columns, great volumes of water, statues, must have Roman scale because, without it, they would look absurd. Having no relation to necessity, to time or to place, classical elements can exalt any authority because they have immediate access to the understanding of all peoples. They are suited to the multi-national or imperial state where national origins are of no importance, and they therefore are very suited to us. We are not a national state in the sense that France, "La Grande Nation," is a national state. Washington, in his wisdom, saw to it that the new Federal city was given the "lingua togata" of design, via L'Enfant and Thornton, a language of design that grasps fully the human bases and the consequent liberties of architectural art.

Roman scale has to do with our apprehension of architectural elements. If we can walk into the fireplace, if the damask has a six-foot repeat, if the balusters are four feet high, if the eggs in an egg-and-dart molding are ostrich size, if a cherub holding up a Holy Water stoup is seven feet high (as at St. Peter's) then we say the scale is big. The scale at the World Trade Center is small because although the building is immense it is made up of bits and pieces reiterated, and the ceilings are low. It is an immense hive as for bees or termites. We have "thoughts that breathe and words that burn," we crave cosmos; we hate death and chaos, "we love the flowers of the field" etc. These are a few samplings of what occasions Grand Manner. As Henry James pointed out (cited on p. 17) the Grand Manner is always simple, but it has scale, noble scale, metaphysical scale, a scale that has nothing to do with necessity (exiguous): you can't have grandeur without it.

Geoffrey Scott, in *The Architecture of Humanism*, says that architecture is the unconscious transcription of the body's states into forms of building, and scale identifies these feelings. At Pennsylvania Station, New York, there was the Grand Concourse, so reminiscent of the tepidarium at the Baths of Caracalla, and with a vault that was one foot higher than the nave of St. Peter's. Leading to the Concourse there was a long vaulted hall of shops reminiscent of Trajan's market or bazaar just behind his Forum. There were screens of columns, and soaring vaults, and great flights of stairs. "Through

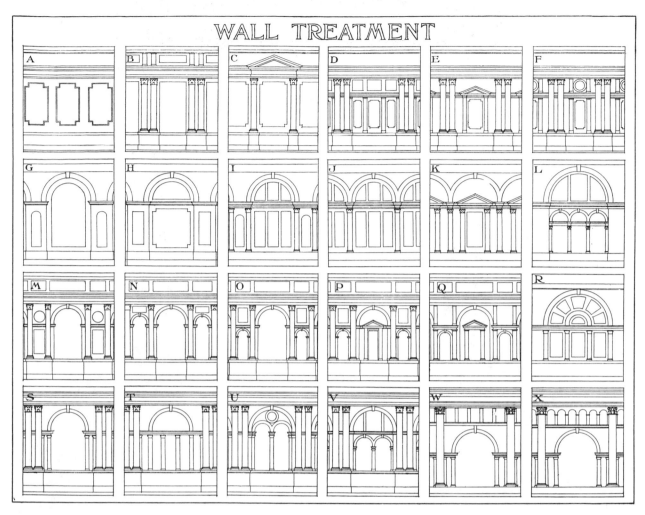

FIG. 4 Wall Treatment. From William R. Ware, *The American Vignola*

these spaces we could perceive ourselves to move; these lines, should we describe them, be our path and our gesture; these masses are capable, like ourselves, of pressure and resistance," wrote Scott. We know the feelings that are aroused by Roman scale. Then there are the feelings aroused, we will say, by the Place Vendôme and the Invalides in Paris, for brevity let us term them regal, and then right down through the hierarchy to the feeling of coziness aroused by a Cape Cod cottage.

The facade (plate 6) and the elements from it were chosen for this book from a multiplicity of examples because Domenico Fontana domesticated the *terribilità* of Michelangelo and made his elements usable. All artists in the generation following Michelangelo were epigoni. Domenico Fontana was the architect for Sixtus V (Peretti). He built the lantern (plate 8) of the dome of St. Peter's after designs by Michelangelo. He moved the obelisk of Nero's circus from its original position to the Piazza San Pietro. He built the palaces of the Lateran and the Quirinale, and of Sixtus V at the Vatican and of the King of Naples. I list these buildings

because I think it is encouraging to think of one's self following in the footsteps of a master.

The cornice shown in Plate 6 is from the Corinthian Order. The whole entablature is just like the Ionic except that the cornice has a modillion band. The band rests on an ovolo molding, in this case decorated with egg-and-dart. The modillions or brackets consist of a double scroll, below which is fixed an acanthus leaf. Homer nods, and in our plate there is a mistake. In the frieze of the corner pier there is a star, and splayed out above it at the prescribed angle of forty-five degrees is the cornice. It can be seen that on either side of the splay in the modillion band there is a modillion seen from the side. The projection does not give room for this. If you will look at the plan you will see that the projection is very slight, and in the plan no such modillion is shown. The soffit of the corona, that is, the underside of the member carried by the modillions, is occupied between modillions by a sinkage with moldings, called a 'caisson' in the middle of which there is usually a rosette, but here there is a Chigi star.

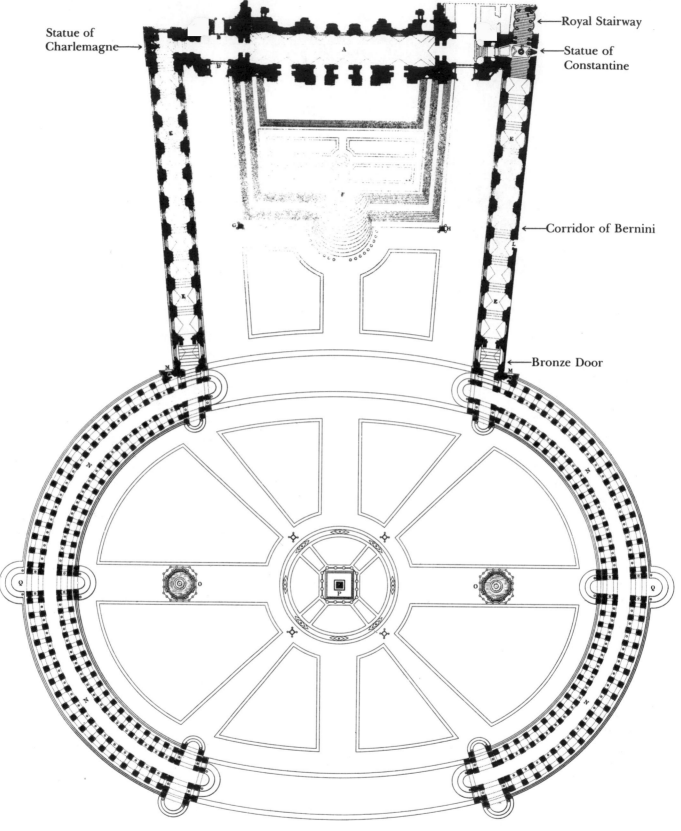

Statue of
Charlemagne

Royal Stairway

Statue of
Constantine

Corridor of Bernini

Bronze Door

(2) PLAN GENERAL DE LA GRANDE PLACE DE LA BASILIQUE DE St PIERRE

(1) Carlo Maderno
(2) Lorenzo Bernini

Chappuis. sc.

10   20   30   40   50ᵐ   60   70   80   90   100 Mètres.

Echelle de 1 mill. pour mètre.

Vᶜ A. MOREL et Cⁱᵉ Editeurs.   Imp. Lamoureux. Paris   72

PLATE 1. Plan of Saint Peter's Square

Armes au dessus des Portiques d'entrée de la Colonnade.

Lorenzo Bernini.

J. Sulpis. sc.

PLATE 2. Interior of the Colonnade of Saint Peter's Square

PLATE 3. The Royal Stairway or *Scala Regia*, the State Entrance to the Pontifical Palace by Bernini with the Statue of Constantine

138

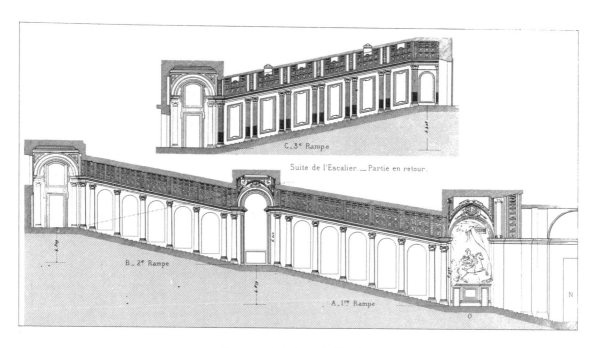

C.. 3e Rampe

Suite de l'Escalier. — Partie en retour.

B.. 2e Rampe

A.. 1re Rampe

N

O

Coupes sur la longueur de l'Escalier.

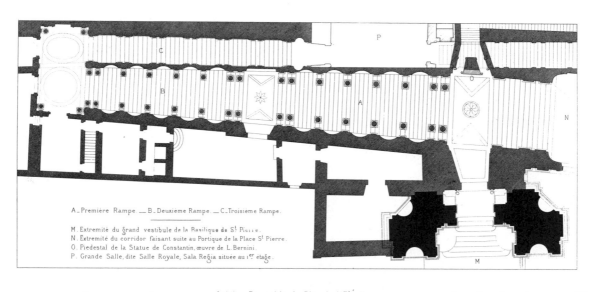

P

C

B

A

O

N

M

A.. Première Rampe. — B.. Deuxieme Rampe. — C.. Troisieme Rampe.

M. Extremité du grand vestibule de la Basilique de St Pierre.
N. Extremité du corridor faisant suite au Portique de la Place St Pierre.
O. Piedestal de la Statue de Constantin, œuvre de L. Bernini.
P. Grande Salle, dite Salle Royale, Sala Regia située au 1er étage.

Ensemble du Plan de l'Escalier.

Echelle de 32 mill. p.r mètre.

Echelle de 4 mill. p.r mètre.

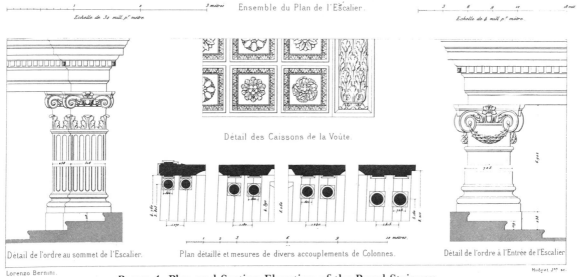

Détail des Caissons de la Voûte.

Détail de l'ordre au sommet de l'Escalier.   Plan détaillé et mesures de divers accouplements de Colonnes.   Détail de l'ordre à l'Entrée de l'Escalier.

Lorenzo Bernini.   Huguet Jne sc.

PLATE 4. Plan and Section Elevation of the Royal Stairway

139

Plate 5. Cross-section of the Portico Looking Left or South with the Statue of Charlemagne at the End.
Above the Portico The Hall of Blessings or *Aula delle Benedizione* with its Very High Ceiling

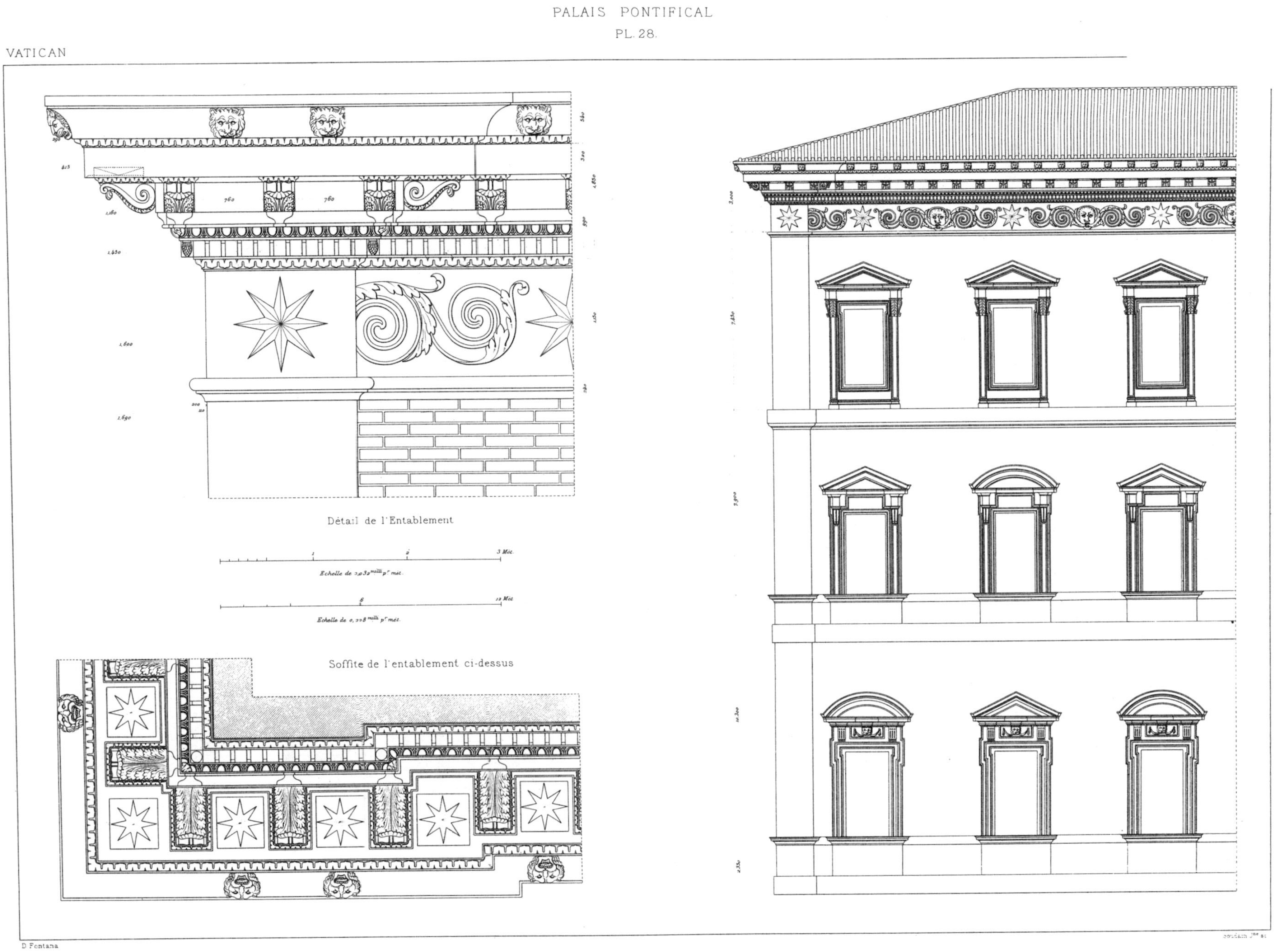
PALAIS PONTIFICAL
PL. 28.
VATICAN
Détail de l'Entablement
Echelle de 0,032 milli p.r mèt.
Echelle de 0,008 milli p.r mèt.
Soffite de l'entablement ci-dessus
D. Fontana

Plate 6. Part of the Facade of the Palace of Sixtus V (Peretti).

VATICAN

PALAIS PONTIFICAL

PL. 29

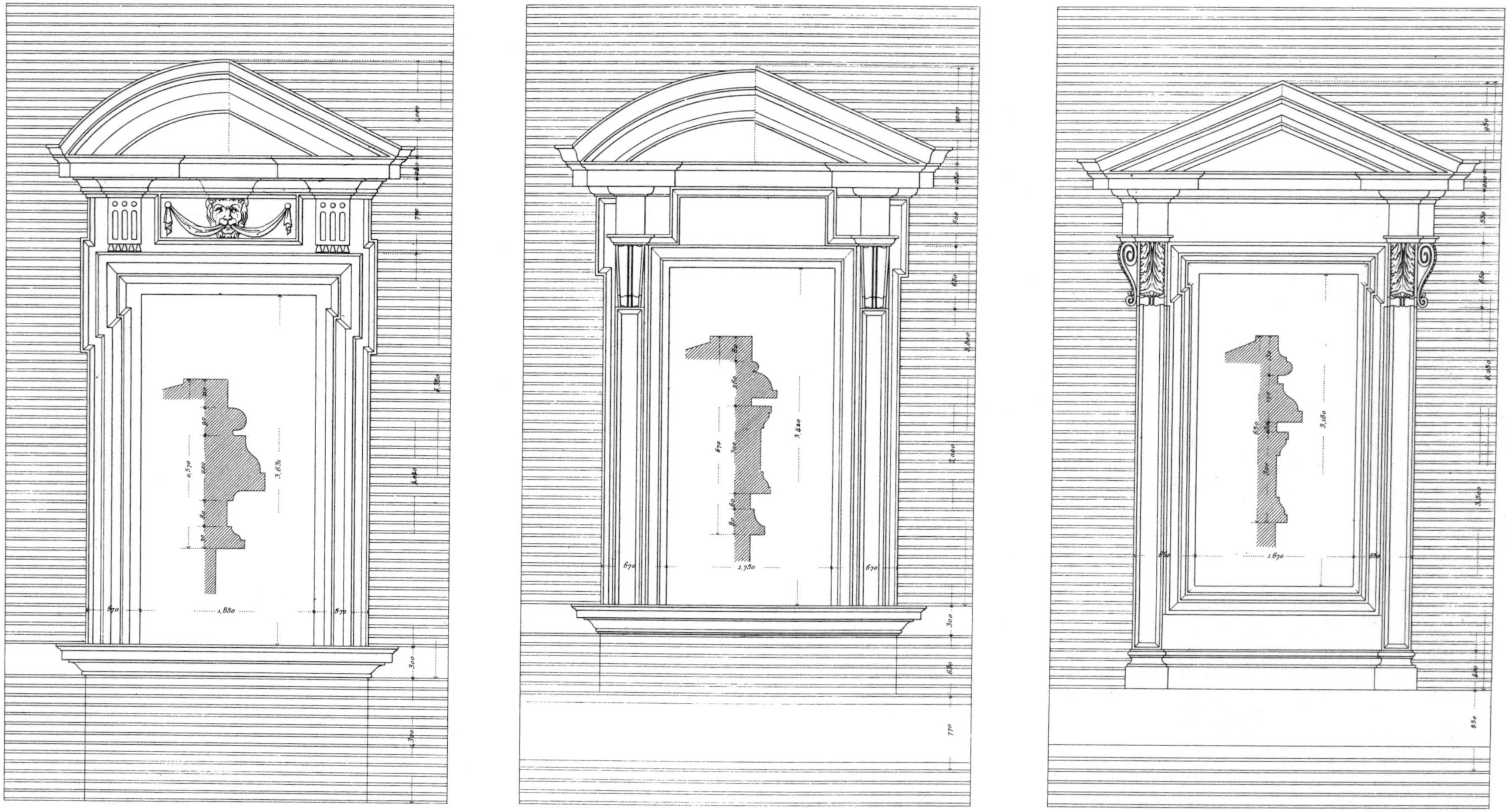

Fenêtres du 1er Etage

Fenêtres du 2e Etage

Echelle de 0,024 milli. pr mètre.

Fenêtres du 3e Etage

N. Les Etages correspondent aux galeries des Loges

.1520.

D. Fontana.

P. Bury sc.

Plate 7. Windows of the Palace of Sixtue V (Peretti)

Ve A. MOREL et Cie Editeurs.

Imp. Lamoureux, Paris. 159

Elévation géométrale de la lanterne de la grande Coupole

PLATE 8. The Lantern of the Great Dome by Domenico Fontana after the Design of Michelangelo

143

XIII · THE VATICAN: GREAT ROOMS

The great lesson, the message to be derived from this memorial room (plate 1), is the value of marble.

Imperial Rome glittered with marble, and yet no marble exists geologically in Rome or the surrounding districts. Ancient Rome's marble was imported, and barges arrived in a never ending stream laden with marbles from the quarries of Greece, Asia, Africa, Spain and France.

The use of marble on a vast scale proves two things. First, the intention to beautify buildings at any cost, and the second, the choice of this particular durable substance as the best means for doing so.

Our cult of the jewel, for its own sake for its arresting of light, was not popular in Antiquity. The Romans adored marble. Magnates went wild over the importation from distant lands of the rarest varieties, and about seven hundred different kinds of marble have been catalogued. Often a particularly rare piece would be shaped into a vase suited to it, in the manner of our cutting and faceting of jewels.

In these two views the columns and pilasters are from Antique sources. Eight thousand Antique marbles still stand in Rome, re-used in churches and palaces. Marbles from ancient sources were used at the Getty villa at Malibu (fig. 1). Here it is pleasant to indulge in reveries. A piece of "Giallo Antico," for example, will muster a pageant of a civilization in which we are but episodes. It is a pale yellow-flushed with a deeper yellow veined with purple. It was quarried in Algeria and rowed across the Mediterranean to Trajan's port of Rome, an hexagonal basin (each side eighteen hundred feet) still in existence, and was fashioned, possibly, into

a column and polished to mirror brilliance and stood giving an authority by reason of its costliness and beauty to some ancient edifice, and it witnessed all the vicissitudes of the Fall of Rome, was buried and then dug up exposed to our gaze. All this gives rise to a train of reflection which is central to the mood of classicism, a pathos which was recognized and made visible in Antique sculpture and painting.

The classical mood deals with the beauty and the loneliness of the human condition, and the sublimity of the timeless order of the cosmos and its complimentary contrast with the brevity of our lives.

Like leaves on trees the race of Man is found.
Now green in youth, now with'ring on the ground,
Another race the following spring supplies
  The Iliad of Homer trans. Alexander Pope

Short is the space of time in which the happiness of mortal men growth up, and even so, doth it fall to the ground, when stricken down by adverse doom. Creatures of a day, what is anyone? What is he not? Man is but a dream of a shadow, but when a gleam of sunshine cometh out, is a gift of heaven, a radiant light resteth on men, aye and a gentle life.

  Pythian Odes. Pindar

In the Gallery of the Candelabra famous pieces have been set before us. Pan removes a thorn from a foot of a satyr, Hellenistic style. Left front an Antique fountain. Water spurted out of the mouths of the sacks on the drawers' backs. Great plinths, great vases. The vases with just grooves or flutes and the columns are in rare colored marbles. Marbles like these are sold today as "marmi degli scavi" (marbles from escavations). The sculptures' vases and plinths would be in marbles of neutral tone and how glorious they are. Acanthuses, seahorses,

Fig. 1 The Main Entrance of the J. Paul Getty Museum in Malibu, 1977. Norman Neuerburg, design consultant. Photo Julius Shulman. Courtesy of J. Paul Getty Museum

masks, birds: I suppose no finer ornaments exist. A marble candlestick from Hadrian's Villa which stands in this gallery was reproduced in bronze as a pair by McKim, Mead & White and they stand on the front staircases of Low Library, Columbia University (fig. 2).

The Hall of the Greek Cross (plate 2) I remember as a glare of colored marble and gilded bronze. The room is dominated by the two imperial sarcophagi in porphyry, an immensely hard igneous marble which can accept a glass-like polish. These are dark purple crimson.

The one on the right was made for Saint Helena, mother of Constantine. On the left is that of Saint Costanza, the daughter of Constantine. It is decorated with symbols of Christianity: Cherubs harvesting grapes, peacocks, sheep and great acanthus spirals which were repeated in the mosaics of her church, Santa Costanza, near Sant'Agnese fuori le Mura where this sarcophagus stood originally.

At the door are two Egyptian telamons in granite from Hadrian's Villa. The door leads into the Sala della Rotonda, the Domed Room. In the middle is a colossal porphyry basin from the Golden House of Nero. On axis we see the eleven-foot tall statue of Hercules in gilded bronze from the Theatre of Pompey (plate 2).

Letarouilly's engraved drawings far surpass any possible photographic representation of this room which is one of the three rooms (plate 3) decorated by Raphael for Julius II who used them as his dwelling place.

On the left wall is "The School of Athens" with Plato, Aristotle, Socrates, Pythagoras, and others. The architecture of the hall is modelled on Bramante's design for St. Peter's and was used in part, the arch to the rear (see p. 100), as an entrance to the exhibition, "Ars in Urbe," held at Yale University Art Gallery in 1953, the opening gun of the classical renascence which is now with us.

On the right wall is a representation of the Christian world. It is divided into Heaven and Earth and they are united to one another by that mystical bond, the sacrament of the Eucharist displayed on the altar. In the upper part the heavenly host is present, and on earth the personages whom the church has most honored for learning and holiness are ranged to either side of the altar.

On the window wall, in the lunette over the window, is a lunette showing an allegory of Prudence and Temperance. To the right of the window is a picture representing Ecclesiastical Law and to the

FIG. 2 Lamp standard in front of Low Library, Columbia University, New York City. Designed in 1898 by McKim, Mead & White. Photo Dick Schuler

146

right Civil Law. Both show events in the remote past, but the figures are portraits of contemporaries of Raphael.

On the ceiling (plate 4) are four round pictures, starting from the left and going clockwise, show Poetry, Theology, Justice and Philosophy. The square pictures refer to the Judgment of Solomon, Original Sin, Astronomy and Apollo and Marsyas.

I have provided this explanation of the room because classical art always tells a story and it is valuable for a mural decorator. This book is not addressed merely to architects to see a cogent scheme. Painters in those days were told what to paint by their patrons who delegated the work to iconographers. A much-used book was Cesare Ripa's *Iconologia*. It is a handbook for personifications for the use of artists, first published in 1593. It was a major source at Versailles.

The floor here (plate 3) is known as Cosmatesque work. This style goes back to the twelfth century, and was never changed. The round discs are made out of Antique columns sawn in sections, and the winding bands and backgrounds are made from small fragments of Antique marble. The predominant colors are green and red. These are porphyry. Whenever you see green porphyry which looks like puree of spinach, or red which is a reddish liver color speckled with pink, you may be sure that they come from Antique buildings as they have never been quarried since.

How would this room have looked when the pope lived here? There would have been a bed in heavily sculptured walnut with gilding and painting, the posts massive and vigorously carved, but not much higher than the headboard. The bed would have stood on a platform. There would have been a few chairs and tables. The chairs richly upholstered in cut velvet with fringes and gilt braid. Furniture in the past was usually kept against the wall and pulled out and placed by the groom of the chambers when in use. There would have been silver lamps and candlesticks on the tables, but the illumination by our standards was nil. The general effect would have been, to our eyes, sparse.

Another *stanza* (plate 5) takes its names from the giant lunette, the Fire in the Borgo. It depicts a story of how Pope Leo III, 795–816, extinguished a fire in the Borgo, the district around St. Peter's, by making the sign of the cross. In the mural's center the pope is shown standing in a loggia designed by Bramante. In the foreground is a scene from the Aeneid which tells of the burning of Troy.

Aeneas is shown carrying his father, Anchises, from the burning city. ("As Aeneas, our great ancestor, did from the flames of Troy upon his shoulder the old Anchises bear," Shakespeare, *Julius Caesar*, I–2.) It evokes the union of Christianity and classical culture, of religion and philosophy, of church and state, of literature and law which is seen throughout so much of the mural decoration of the Vatican.

The mural decorations of the *stanze* are works which, in power of representation, have never been surpassed. Raphael, in telling his stories, made use of his great formal sense to create memorable symbols of the basic doctrines of the Christian Church. In executing them he provided a logical system of classical composition. This ability, which has made Raphael the primary source of all subsequent academic art and which has done his reputation no good when the academic is at a discount, enabled him in a short life-time to achieve an astonishing output thanks to his power of delegating much of the preparatory work to highly trained studio assistants.

As Kenyon Cox observed in *The Classic Point of View* he was "the greatest master of formal design that the world has ever seen, and he gave us the still unequalled models of decorative composition . . . In one room, the Stanza della Segnatura . . . , he has given us the perfect examples of composition for the circular medallion, the rectangular panel, the semicircular lunette, and the pierced lunette, or lunette with an opening cut through it . . ."

The first sketches of the rooms of Nero's Golden House were made about 1491. The Baths of Titus had been built over them, and they were filled with earth up to the springing of the arches. As they were called "grottos" or caves, the style of their decoration was called "grotesque," a term usually applied today to forms associated with the Gothic or to those distorted and unnatural combinations, quaint to disgusting.

The style of decoration of the rooms with slender-columned pavilions, garlands, birds, griffons, arabesques, etc. fascinated Raphael and Giovanni da Udine. ". . . They were both seized with astonishment," according to Vasari. However, "the small scale and fine detail of this style were appropriate to the modest rooms of Roman villas such as those of Pompeii and Herculaneum. Here in the vast halls of Nero's palace it is difficult not only to appreciate, but even to see their delicate fantasy," wrote

Margaret Scherer in *Marvels of Ancient Rome*. So, it is perhaps as well that the chambers were filled with earth to the imposts of the arches for our visiting artists, otherwise by candlelight the vaults would have been invisible.

The style of the Loggias is far richer and Letarouilly's engravers have given us a very useful picture of it (plate 6).

Bramante built loggias around the Court of Saint Damasus or of the Loggias (directly north of the Scala Regia, see Chapter X, plate 1) which are used as access-ways to the rooms of the palace. The decorations here are outside the apartment decorated for Pope Julis II. Of the fifty-two subjects shown, forty-eight are from the Old Testament, with only the four last being from the Gospel as an appropriate introduction to the pictures which celebrate the foundation and triumphs of the Church to be found in the adjoining *Stanze*.

In small rooms Raphael kept more strictly to Roman principles of ornament as seen in the grisaille work behind the shutters in the Room of the Fire in the Borgo (plate 7), but when he came to the huge field of the loggias he used greater freedom in developing a new and more complex syntax emphasizing and enhancing, in a vision of luxurious refined elegance, the many interconnecting partitions of the thirteen arches, vaulted cupolas, niches, windows, lunettes, undersides of the arches, combining stucco and gilding with painting (plates 6 and 8). The grotesques and antiquity-inspired stuccoes now became an architectural composition whose architectural distribution is reminiscent of the Colosseum. (The art of the grotesques, especially in the form of candlesticks, had already found expression in the 15th century.)

The Hall of Masks (plate 9) is the kind of room which can be seen in most palaces and villas. There are four doors. Two are false and serve as niches.

Between the doors are niches, and there are niches on the other walls. The niches are built out from the walk and are flanked by columns. There is a heavy cornice and a coved ceiling.

This formula can be applied on even the smallest scale. Here in this country we must abandon the coved ceiling except when we are building "da nuovo." Our great expansion of white ceiling, nobody, not even Edith Wharton and Ogden Codman, Jr. in *The Decoration of Houses* have ever been able to do much about. The "innocents abroad" look at ceilings, but the innocents at home ignore them.

This formula can be put into a New York apartment, say, with ten-foot ceilings. But please do not try to use stock columns and pilasters, everything in a classical scheme is done proportionally, and there is even an instrument called a "proportion divider" to assist the designer in this work.

Now let me briefly mention some of the objects in the room to provide that Roman enticement, the beguilement, the *fond* (translation- essence, background, backdrop, theatre, ground) *romain* which once one has been taken over by it—at first one resists—confers a confraternity which it is very pleasant to belong to.

How agreeable it is to meet another member, you have so many things in common. It is not an exclusive group, quite the opposite. Our gonfalon is really humility. The professor enters St. Peter's. "Oh yes, bees. That's for Barberini," and there are knowing chuckles from students of art history courses. When T. S. Eliot came into the Basilica he fell to his knees overcome by the sanctity and majesty of the place. In Rome "self" becomes unimportant. Having been said, this it must be contradicted in the sense that all Romans and neo-Romans feel superior to everyone else and are always on the "ready to civilize the rude unpolished world." All other places are provincial.

Michel Angelo Simonetti   Hibon sc.

PLATE 1. View of the Gallery of the Candelabra in the Pio Clementino Museum

PLATE 2. View of the Hall of the Greek Cross in the Pio Clementino Museum

PLATE 3. *Stanza della Segnatura*, one of the Raphael Rooms or *Stanze* di Raffaello

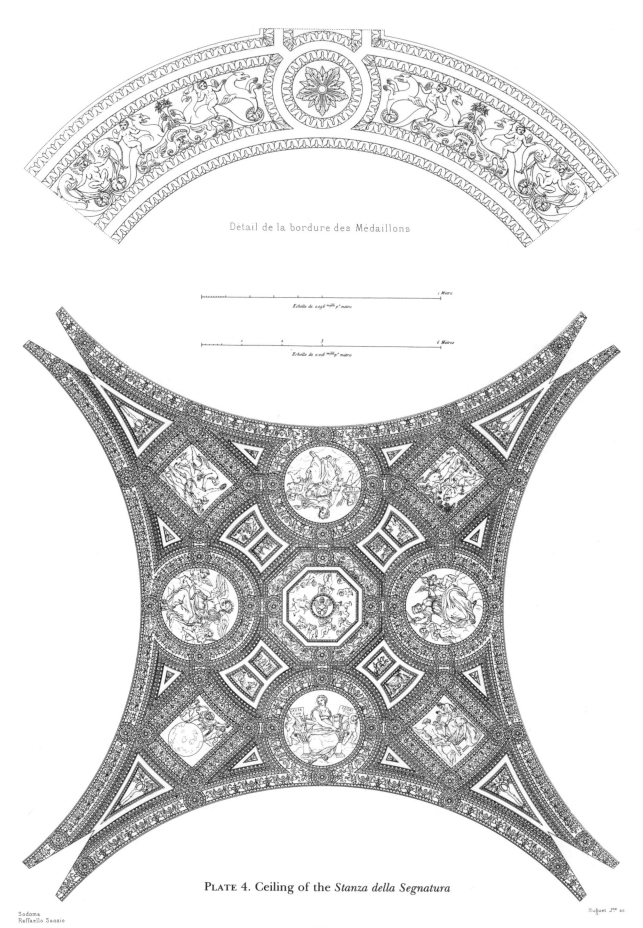

Detail de la bordure des Médaillons

1 Mètre

Echelle de 0.096 milli pr mètre.

6 Mètres

Echelle de 0.016 milli pr mètre.

PLATE 4. Ceiling of the *Stanza della Segnatura*

Sodoma
Raffaello Sanzio

Huguet Jne sc.

152

PLATE 5. Room of the Fire in the Borgo, *Stanza del Incendio del Borgo*, one of the Raphael Rooms

153

Plate 6. Details of two of the Pilasters in the Raphael Loggias on the Court of Saint Damasus or of the Loggias

154

Polidoro da Caravaggio. Echelle de 124 Milli. pour Mètre 1 Mètre Pralon lith

PLATE 7. Grisaille Painting Behind the Shutters in the Room of the Fire in the Borgo

155

PLATE 8. Decoration in the Raphael Loggias

156

Michel-Angelo Simonetti
Domenico del Angeli.

Hibon et Sellier sc.

Vᵉ A. MOREL et Cⁱᵉ Editeurs

Imp. Lamoureux Paris 155

PLATE 9. Hall of Masks called *Il Gabinetto* in the Pio Clementino Musem